1968

TWO DRAMAS

TWO DRAMAS
PAUL CLAUDEL

BREAK OF NOON
Partage de Midi

THE TIDINGS BROUGHT TO MARY
L'Annonce faite à Marie

translations and introductions
WALLACE FOWLIE

Henry Regnery Company—Chicago—1960

CONTENTS

TWO DRAMAS OF CLAUDEL

Foreword

A French public, eager to attend performances of Claudel's plays, has gradually grown up during the past twenty years. The Barrault production of *Le Soulier de Satin* at the Comédie-Francaise in 1943, and the Barrault production of *Tete d'Or* at the Théâtre de France in 1959, mark the limits of this period during which the playwright reached a recognition he had not known before the war.

In publishing these two plays in the same volume, it is not the intention of the translator and publisher merely to present examples of a secular play (*Partage de Midi*) and a religious play (*L'Annonce faite à Marie*), and hence indicate the diversity of this playwright's art. Rather it is the hope to demonstrate in these two texts the unity of Claudel's understanding of the world and of man's action in the world. Whether it be the trial of passion (as in *Break of Noon*) or the trial of mystical love (as in *The Tidings Brought to Mary*), this poet is concerned with illuminating the transcendent greatness of such trials. Man's physical commitments and the earthiness of his world are in both of these dramas. But the characters of the dramas are ready, when the moment comes, to be violated by the Spirit.

WALLACE FOWLIE

BREAK OF NOON

Ω

INTRODUCTION

1. Claudel and Barrault

In June 1939, Jean-Louis Barrault visited Claudel in Brangues, the poet's home in Savoie, for the express purpose of asking permission to produce three plays, not one of which had been performed professionally at that time. After naming the three titles: *Tête d'Or*, the earliest play, written when Claudel was twenty, *Partage de Midi*, written after a personal crisis in the life of the poet when he was thirty-two, and *Le Soulier de Satin*, the last play, written when Claudel was in his fifties, Barrault was asked to explain the reasons for his choice. His answer demonstrated a good understanding of the three difficult texts. *Tête d'Or*, he said has the still unformed power of the later plays. Barrault used the image of sap: "*Tête d'Or* est votre sève." *Partage de Midi* he called the trial or the test (*l'épreuve*) of the playwright. And *Le Soulier* he called the synthesis (*votre synthèse*). Claudel,

[3]

at the time of this visit, was unmoved by Barrault's arguments and critical justifications, and he refused permission. He claimed that *Tête d'Or* had become unreadable ("*Tête d'Or* est devenu illisible."). For *Partage de Midi*, he said he would not give his authorization, and this seemed to be for personal reasons. *Le Soulier de Satin* he claimed was too long for theatrical performance.

Barrault's great belief in Claudel helped him to persevere. He waited for a few years and then seized the first real opportunity, in 1943, during the German Occupation of Paris, when he was called to the Comédie-Française, to put on the first production of *Le Soulier de Satin*, the third of the plays he had previously asked for. The success of this production unquestionably influenced Claudel in granting permission to Barrault to put on, in 1948, in his own theatre of the Marigny, *Partage de Midi*. And finally, in the 1959-60 season, four years after the death of the poet, Barrault put on *Tête d'Or*, the first of his productions as the new director of the Théâtre de France (formerly the Odéon).

So, the order in the productions of these three plays is the reverse of the order of their composition. And all three productions are the work of Jean-Louis Barrault. The opening of *Partage de Midi*, in December 1948, was a spectacular event, an homage to Claudel by Barrault's company and by a brilliant audience. Barrault himself as Mesa, if he did not physically resemble Claudel at the turn of the century, gave to the lines a rhythm and a resonance that would have been hard to match. Claudel himself has spoken of the striking appearance of Edwige Feuillère in the role of Ysé. On the stage of the Marigny, during rehearsals and performances in 1948, Edwige Feuillère as Ysé was the reincarnation for Claudel of the woman who in his own life, in 1900, had created the personal drama of which *Partage de Midi* was the first literary expression.

2. *Claudel and his play*

The literary genesis of the play is to be found in two texts, in the last part of the ode *Les Muses*, and in the page-long poem *Ténèbres*. In the single poem *Ténèbres*, the drama itself is formulated and its spiritual resolution as well.

The poet himself speaks in *Ténèbres* and says that he is here and the one he loves is in some other place, and the silence between them is awesome.

[5]

*Je suis ici, l'autre est ailleurs, et le silence est
terrible.*

The poem is about this absence and this separation. The symbol of darkness, of night, is this
absence of communication, and the growing horror which fills the soul of the poets.

*Je prête l'oreille, et je suis seul, et la terreur
m'envahit.*

He speaks of hearing the resemblance of the
beloved's voice and the sound of a cry. And the
reader accepts the strange fact that this cry
comes from a great distance, even from another
continent. In his loneliness, the poet walks from
one wall to the other of his room. He knows
that the temptation which fills his heart is insti-
gated by the Prince of the World, but he knows
also that where sin abounds, there also the mercy
of God abounds to an even richer degree.

*Je sais que là où le péché abonde, là Votre
miséricorde surabonde.*
*Il faut prier, car c'est l'heure du Prince du
monde.*

This poem of *Ténèbres* is a single cry, but so
full and so swift that it carries the weight of

[6]

Partage de Midi. In a form even more radically reduced, are the two words of St. Augustine which serve as epigraph to *Le Soulier de Satin: etiam peccata.* Even sins are of some use in the indecipherable economy with which God orders the world.

Closer still to the literal drama of *Partage de Midi* is the final passage of *Les Muses,* first of the *Cinq Grandes Odes.* The two dates, appended to *Les Muses*: Paris, 1900 and Foutchéou, 1904, indicate the primacy of this text. The major elements of the first act are sketched in the last two pages of the ode: the woman whom the poet meets on the deck of a ship,

O mon amie sur le navire!

and the fire of passion which the two of them were to experience on the ship:

*Nous allions retrouver la même conflagration
Nourrie de tout le présent bondé, la Troie du
    monde réel en flammes!*

Even the blond hair of the woman is evoked and the new role of muse which she becomes for the poet as she stands in the sea wind, on the prow of a boat.

[7]

Toi-même, amie, tes grands cheveux blonds
dans le vent de la mer . . .
O mon amie! ô Muse dans le vent de la mer!
ô idée chevelue à la proue!

This meeting between the poet and the woman he will first call "Muse" and then "Ysé," came at a moment in his life which he describes both in this final passage of the ode and in *Partage de Midi* where the poet is called Mesa. The writing of the work and the first meager edition of 150 copies (1906) were, then, the exteriorization of a personal drama.

When, in 1948, almost half a century after the personal experience and the writing of the first version of *Partage de Midi*, Claudel acceded to the request of Barrault, he began work on a new version of the play for the Marigny production. The early text seemed imperfect to him and far too personal. A veritable collaboration took place between the poet and the director. Gradually during the months of revision and early rehearsals, *Partage de Midi* grew into a new work for Claudel. The long passage of time had resolved the initial dilemma in his life. The rewriting of the play made it into a work of importance for him. Barrault's understanding of the text,

[8]

the constant consultations with him on problems of *mise-en-scène* and interpretation, the appearance of Edwige Feuillère as Ysé and the physical resemblance she bore with the woman whom Claudel had met on the deck of the *Ernest Simons*, helped him to understand what had happened fifty years earlier and to complete the acting version of the play.

Actually two new versions were written by Claudel. The first, written for Barrault and used by him in the 1948 production, has just been published for the first time in volume 11 of the *Oeuvres Complètes*. The second, completed when rehearsals had begun, is a further modification, especially of act III, and the text which Claudel looked upon as definitive. This is the text used as the basis for the English translation. Barrault was reluctant to incorporate the newer changes and Claudel did not insist.

3. The title and the names

For a Frenchman the title *Partage de Midi* is striking and suggestive. For a Frenchman who is unfamiliar with the play itself, the title has little specific connotation, although it is thoroughly satisfying in an aesthetic sense. For a Frenchman who knows the play, the title provides a cluster

of meanings, all related and all mutually suggestive. Behind the poet's title, *Partage de Midi*, is
a familiar geological term in French, *le partage
des eaux*, which refers to the divisioning of rain
on a mountain top when the water is separated
and flows down two sides.

The general meaning of *Partage de Midi* is
that of a separation or of a turning point. The
poet of *Les Muses* designates himself in the ode
as a new man, a new poet who has been transformed by some crisis. The first part of the ode
was written in 1900 when at the Benedictine
monasteries of Solesmes and Ligugé, Paul Claudel
tested his religious vocation. The answer to this
test was negative and Claudel accepted the decision of his spiritual directors. The invocation
to Erato in *Les Muses*, the scene on the boat I
have referred to, was written in 1901 and con-
temporary with *Partage de Midi*. I wish it had
been possible to keep the French title in the
English translation. "Divide of Noon" occurred
to me first as a possibility, but it is too peaceful
for the dramatic connotation of *Partage de Midi*.
This aspect of the title is perhaps better carried
over into "Break of Noon." The French word
midi denotes time and place and passion. (*Le
démon du midi*, for example, is a phrase coined

[10]

by Paul Bourget to describe carnality.) "Transfiguration of Noon" would perhaps be a fuller translation, but I prefer the short simple word "Break" to the long Latin vocable.

The meaning of *midi* as the middle or turning-point was so fixed in the mind of Claudel, that it is audible in each of the names of his characters. *Ysé* in Greek means "equality," *isos*. *Mesa* means "the half." *A-mal-ric* is the divisioning into three. *De Ciz* is "the cutting off." The life of each of these four characters has reached the point of noon in a symbolic sense. They come together on the deck of a boat, but each is isolated from the others, and on the verge of understanding a very profound aspect of his existence. The fact that the boat itself is in the middle of the Indian Ocean is significant. As in a classical tragedy, there is no well-defined scene or setting. What counts is the precise moment in a life time which all four have reached. The destiny of all four is going to undergo a change at the precise moment of noon, which is the conclusion of act I.

4. *The acts and the characters*

The three acts take place in three different settings, and in three different "climates." The

woman Ysé dominates all three acts but plays a
different role in each one. She is the adventuress
in the first act. Three men surround her on the
deck of the ship: her husband De Ciz, a former
lover Amalric, and Mesa whom she has just met
and who is to become her lover. She is desired by
all three men. Easily and deliberately she has
subjugated all three by the curtain line of act I.
At three moments during the course of the act,
the ship's bell rings: four times when the curtain
goes up, six times when Ysé says the line, "Mesa,
I am Ysé." And eight times at the end of the
act which marks noon.

In act II, in the old cemetery of Hong Kong,
Ysé plays the role of lover and seductress. Mesa
takes possession of her at one specific moment in
the action, but the irresistible power she exerts
over him never diminishes while they are together
on the stage. Their four hands intertwined at the
end of the act, state the bond of adultery, a form
of sacrilege sworn to before an old cross which
had been found among the tombs.

Ysé, in act III, is the wife, the woman charac-
terized by fidelity, even if this fidelity is to her
lover. This is the act of the abandoned pagoda.
A Chinese chair, large enough for two persons,
and shaped in the form of an Omega, is the

object—the throne on which the sacrifice is to take place. When he was a student Claudel had been deeply affected by a picture he had come across in Duruy's *Histoire Romaine*, representing an Etruscan funeral throne where the husband and wife stood stiffly beside one another.

Of the three men who surrounded Ysé, Amalric is the physical lover, the sensualist who is bored by any reference to God as a force who might count in a love affair. The world would call Amalric the normal man who enjoys the power of sexuality and who quickly recovers from its obsession when his senses have been satisfied.

In contrast with Amalric, the physical appearance of the husband De Ciz has little importance. He would be unprepossessing in appearance. He would be the male insect. But it is highly important for the audience to realize that De Ciz is sexually endowed, that he has been throughout his marriage the exciting and gifted sexual partner.

Partage de Midi is the martyrdom of Mesa. The center of the play's action is in him. Earlier he had received a call to the priesthood. Temperamentally he was not prepared for such a vocation and he was rejected by the ecclesiastical authorities. He himself was convinced that the negative answer had come from God as well as from his religious superiors. He had been eliminated and his exile had begun. During the first act, on the deck of the boat, we witness the end of this exile and this solitude. At the "break of noon," a fire, rather than illuminating Mesa and Ysé, consumes them. The salvation he had sought in the monastery has changed to a form of damnation in the love he conceives for Ysé.

When we first see Mesa, he is a virgin who has never known a woman. Ysé has no feeling or understanding for the religious drama he has just gone through. But she is fully aware of the traits of his character. He represents for her the lowest, the meanest aspects of the bourgeois-pharisee. He is miserly and egotistical. There is a self-satisfied primness about him, a stubborn self-involvement which is unpleasant. Ysé will provide the force of attraction which his life needs. She is the instrument which will cause him finally to prefer someone else to himself.

5. The meaning of the play

On a television broadcast in 1951, Jean Amrouche interviewed Claudel and asked him if a specific woman and a specific love had been the source of *Partage de Midi*. Claudel answered yes to this direct question and said that the subject had been intimate and confidential, but that the work itself had represented a transformation. Especially in the 1948 versions he wrote for the stage, the poet felt he had reached an understanding of his personal experience. During that year of constant collaboration with Barrault, the play itself took on a tremendous importance for him. He claimed that his entire life was in it, that the play was much more than a literary exercise.

The play is about the meaning of love, and especially about the role of woman in the experience of love. The principal theme can be stated quite simply. An experience of carnality is not sufficient to join a man and a woman. In this experience each possesses the key to the other. But each understands finally that carnality is not that key. Ysé is not happiness for Mesa, but she is there in his life in the place of happiness. Their long scene in the second act is a love duet strongly reminiscent of the love duet in the second act of *Tristan*. The woman becomes in this scene the means by which man will understand the concept of paradise.

The tawdriness of the situation, the easy virtue

[15]

of Ysé, the stock bourgeois temperament of Mesa are mysteriously changed and transformed. In order to make this central action of the play more dramatic, Claudel in rewriting his original version, added many touches of vulgarity, especially in the character of Ysé. In the new version of the second act, the husband De Ciz has no scruples in pushing his wife into the arms of a man who is promising to help him. Claudel understood that the most important element of his play was the realization which comes to Mesa that someone else exists in the world outside of him. He and Ysé are not in the least the romantic couple. When the illumination of love comes to them, it will precipitate them toward catastrophe.

The revision of the third act offered the greatest difficulties. The long solo speech of Mesa at the end of the play, called *Le cantique de Mésa*, had been learned and rehearsed by Barrault before Claudel completed the final version in which he very drastically reduced this monologue and altered it. Claudel urged the acceptance of this final draft of the end, which had actually gone through three or four versions, but Barrault refused.

Up to the ending of the play, *Partage de Midi* (in the words of Amalric) resembles a poker game in which four players are around a table. But there is an invisible Player. And at the end, when Ysé returns, the play becomes clearly the drama of passion. This passion finds its conclusion in suffering and death, and in something beyond death.

6. *Partage de Midi* and *Le Soulier de Satin*

If *Partage de Midi* of 1906 is the first literary expression of a significant personal drama in the life of Claudel, *Le Soulier de Satin* (first published in 1930), is the fuller and more resolved literary expression of the same experience twenty years later. Both plays have the double theme of adultery and the spiritual struggle between the Creator and the creature. Both plays have the same climate of tragedy.

Catholicism is so much a part of the genius of Claudel, his spirit conformed so precisely to Roman orthodoxy in its universal character, that for any clear understanding of the action of these plays, it seems necessary to look upon God as the invisible Actor, the Impresario who can and does use human passion, all degrees and all kinds of human passion, for the realization of His own goal.

[17]

In several of the letters Claudel wrote to André Gide, especially those of 1909, he emphasizes the specific Christian drama of man as opposed, for example, to the drama of man in antiquity. During the life of the Christian, his salvation is never assured once and for all. The Christian has to strive for a daily salvation. Day after day for the believer the struggle that goes on between the visible and the invisible has all the characteristics for Claudel of tragedy. Man is in danger of tragedy at every moment. The Christian life, for Claudel, is a constant state of conflict.

The poet has often said, with the seeming arbitrariness and rigor for which he has been castigated, that only the Christian knows the full experience of desire. In such a statement, he implies that the Christian, when he is fully aware of the metaphysics of his faith, knows in the experience of desire what he really desires. For such a man, what is often called human tragedy, can never be thus limited. It inevitably moves into the dimensions of a cosmic tragedy when centuries form the setting and all of humanity the actors. This conception of tragedy is implicit in the most mysterious scenes of *Le Soulier de Satin* and in the final scene of *Partage de Midi*.

WALLACE FOWLIE

PRINCIPAL EDITIONS OF
Partage de Midi

1906　Written in 1905. Original edition in Paris, at the Bibliothèque de L'Occident. 150 copies.

1948　Mercure de France. The original text, with a preface by Paul Claudel.

1949　Gallimard. The revised text, called "Nouvelle version pour la scène."
(This was used for the English translation.)

1957　Gallimard. Volume XI of the *Oeuvres Complètes*.
This volume contains the version used by Barrault in his production of 1948. It is called "Version pour la scène" and preceded the edition of 1949.

FIRST PERFORMANCE

1948   Théâtre Marigny, Paris. Compagnie Madeleine Renaud—Jean-Louis Barrault. 17 December. Direction by J.-L. Barrault. Settings by Félix Labisse. Costumes by Christian Bérard.

CAST

YSÉ	Edwige Feuillère
MESA	Jean-Louis Barrault
DE CIZ	Jacques Dacqmine
AMALRIC	Pierre Brasseur

ACT I

DRAMATIS PERSONAE

YSÉ

MESA

DE CIZ

AMALRIC

The Indian Ocean. The forward deck of a liner bound for the Far East. Mesa and Amalric are down stage. Ysé and De Ciz are up stage. They appear as if photographed in the midst of a conversation. The bell strikes four times (ten o'clock in the morning). Movement is resumed.

AMALRIC: My good friend, you let them get around you.

MESA: Nothing has been settled yet.

AMALRIC: Then don't settle it. Take my word! I like you, Mesa. Everyone likes you. Don't do it!

MESA: But the deal seems rather promising.

AMALRIC: What about the man who's behind it?

MESA: He has some good sides to his nature.

AMALRIC: I detest weak men, and I don't trust them. Give in if you wish. Just take that fine fellow with you, and it will be as if you are holding an uncorked bottle of seltzer water, a narrow-necked bottle of soda water you don't

[23]

know where to put down. They say he is going to move into your place, with his entire
household. I once knew a fellow like that. He
was called Bernard the hermit crab.[1] The entire household, including the wife. And by
the way, Mesa, what do you think of the wife?

[*Ysé and De Ciz come down stage.*]

YSÉ [*reading the name on an over-elaborate
rocking-chair. She turns to Mesa.*]: Mesa! Does
this beautiful gold rocking-chair belong to
you?

AMALRIC: It would be more accurate to say
that Mesa belongs to the rocking-chair. It has
a sign: DO NOT USE!

MESA: There was no other way of getting rid of
that good-for-nothing[2] who sold it to me.

YSÉ: Will you allow me to use it a bit from time
to time? Just a little bit?

DE CIZ: Ysé! You shouldn't ask such favors.

YSÉ: You see, we were coming from Harrar, and
there was just time to embark at Aden with our
luggage and a servant and the children who
had to be taken care of. We didn't have time
to get a thing.

MESA [*grumpy*]: Of course, you can! As much
as you like!

DE CIZ: As much as you like! Well, Sir, I can

tell you, you won't be in your fine gold rocking-chair very often!

AMALRIC: It won't be hard on him. He never uses it. He is always walking from one end of the boat to the other, and rubbing his hands!

YSÉ: I love to walk, too! This morning we took a long walk together. The coolest hour of the day. It's ridiculous to let the sun rise all alone. Félicien, mon chéri, I shouldn't be surprised if this gentleman were a poet!

DE CIZ: Don't listen to her! She says everything that comes into her head.

YSÉ: It's such a pleasure to meet intelligent people. You've made me live for such a long time with savages!

DE CIZ: Rimbaud wasn't a savage.[3]

YSÉ: Oh! that Rambaud of yours!

DE CIZ: Rimbaud. Arthur Rimbaud. He was my partner in Harrar. I left him my business.

YSÉ: The leather business. You have raw hide and hide not raw. Salted hides and hides not salted. The non-salted hides have the best smell.

AMALRIC: Probably with a little smuggling of fire-arms, as the main business.

YSÉ: I never knew such an idiotic man! There are magnificent sunsets at Harrar. Oh! as far as sunsets go, Harrar has no rival. In fact, they are about the only diversion we have. I used to go into ecstasy, and sometimes I would say to him: "Now come, Rimbaud, give me an answer, isn't that beautiful?" But he would never reply and just look at me with his eyes of an idiot. He would look first at the sun, and then at me.

DE CIZ: You exaggerate. In business matters he was no fool.

YSÉ: He isn't like Mesa. Tell me, is it all right just to call you Mesa. Me-sa! [*She sings on two notes.*] When I think of all the things you told me about Lakshmi and the soft part of the inner arm! Tell them about it, Mesa!

MESA [*deliberately pedantic*]: Lakshmi is the wife of Brahma. She is painted in blue in the midst of a green rainbow.

YSÉ: Yes, green. You understand it is because of the sea which was all rose-color that he said that. All rose!

MESA: Not only rose. There is a delightful tint of sulphur, too.

YSÉ: Of course, sulphur! As in the small of the arm. On the flesh of the small of the arm. A woman's arm, naturally. Mesa here is an expert on the subject of the flesh of a woman's arm.

[26]

[*She bursts out laughing. De Ciz and Mesa are visibly irritated.*]

AMALRIC: It's a good idea to take an early morning walk on the deck. I was there, too. I saw you at a distance. Not too far off.

YSÉ: I love walking barefoot in cold water with the sand grating and scratching under the soles of my feet when they're washing the deck. I should mention the eyes too. What was that quotation he gave? "Her eyes" . . .⁴ Yes, I should mention the eyes too.

    [*She closes her eyes, opens them, and closes one.*]

MESA: I don't remember.

DE CIZ: She is mad. Pay no attention to her! [*To Ysé*] I wish you'd attend to the luggage. The boat is in total confusion because of the party they're preparing for tonight.

MESA: A party? Good! That means that today the boat belongs just to us. Very pleasant indeed.

    [*He rubs his hands.*]

DE CIZ: Ysé, I insist that I need you.

    [*He goes down the stairway.*]

YSÉ: I'm coming! I'm flying! [*She waves her arms as if they were wings.*] But don't you leave! I'm coming back! I forbid your stirring

from this spot. I'm coming back in a moment.
[*She disappears.*]

AMALRIC: A charming woman!

YSÉ [*reappearing and declaiming*]: "Her eyes
are of another color. The sea changes color like
the eyes of a woman you hold in your arms."
[*She laughs and disappears, then reappears.*]
And I forbid your using my rocking-chair.
"Her eyes like the eyes of a woman you take
in your arms!"
[*She disappears.*]

AMALRIC: Well! Isn't it true she is charming?

MESA: You must understand that I don't know
very much about women.

AMALRIC: That I can believe! And the ladies
will never know very much about you. But
I like you and I understand you. Better than
you think I do! I am certain that she loves me.
Yet you are attractive to her. It is strange, for
she is afraid of you! And she is always wanting
to know what you think of her. It's hard on
me, don't you think?

MESA: I think she is a brazen-faced flirt.

AMALRIC: That's a ridiculous phrase to use.
You know nothing about the subject. Mon
cher, she is a magnificent woman.

MESA: Ever since we left Aden, you haven't stopped telling me that over and over.

AMALRIC: Well, it's a fact! And you don't seem to realize it. Even if you are absent-minded, I think at last I have put the idea into your head. That scene you two had the other evening, you remember? And that cigarette she gave you— you who don't smoke—how devoutly you smoked it all! Come, don't be embarrassed!

MESA: You're a fool!

AMALRIC: Dear fellow, I might as well tell you, I go only for blonds. She isn't a flirt. Look out for yourself! She's a warrior, a conqueror! She has to dominate and tyrannize, or else give herself awkwardly like some large prancing animal! She is a thoroughbred mare, and it would amuse me to mount her if I had the time. But she has no rider, and with her colts which follow her about, she runs like a naked horse. I see her stampeding, breaking everything and injuring herself. She is a foreigner, here in our midst, separated from her home and her land. She is a leader's wife, in the sense that she needs heavy duties to hold her down, a large gold horse-cloth. But this husband of hers, this handsome son, the effete man from

[29]

southern France with his tender eyes, the low-down engineer and poor double-dealer, you can easily see that he is a vice for her. All he has done is give her children. It is terrifying to see them all on their way to China. They've made up their minds about you, Mesa. You can believe me! Bernard the hermit crab. The entire family of Bernard the hermit crab, esquire. Here they come.

> [*Ysé returns and behind her comes De Ciz, burdened with various objects he lays down on the deck.*]

YSÉ: It bores this husband of mine to get my things. He's very displeased. But I am happy to be going forward. Forward! En avant! I wish we would never arrive! Why isn't he happy? He always seems to be pretending to smile. But I am happy! [*She laughs. Mesa and De Ciz both seem irritated.*] Perhaps you would like it better if I weren't happy? But I am, and there's nothing you can do about it.

MESA: You are happy and Amalric is content.

DE CIZ: Because he's successful.

AMALRIC: Me? I was cleaned out last year. Rinsed like a beer glass, by God! [5] I am beginning all over.

MESA: He's happy because he is needed.

AMALRIC: No, it's simply because I am busy. There are many things which I need, and many things for which I am needed.

YSÉ: Amalric, you will succeed. You are skillful with your hands. What you do, you do well. I like a man who can use his hands.

MESA: Yes, a cow would let herself be milked by those hands.

DE CIZ: He is in full control of his own powers. He is sure of his place under every circumstance!

YSÉ: And there is no place for me anywhere. For the past ten years my household and my home have been a chaise longue tied on to a trunk and a bunch of keys in my bag.

MESA [*pointing to the sun*]: Our home? There is our home, fellow wanderers! Its light is strong enough and we get on together, don't we? Look at him, look at our master up there, with his millions of rays, quite unconcerned with the earth, like an old woman busy with the stitches of her crochet-hook!

YSÉ: He is too strong for me! I wish night would come! I am like an animal that lives only at night.

AMALRIC: The full strength of the sun is like the full strength of one's life! It is good to be

[31]

able to face everything, death and all the rest. I am strong enough to hold out against it.

MESA: In a few minutes it will be noon in the heavens, noon at the center of our lives. And we are here together, around the same age of our instant, midway in the full horizon, free, taken out of our boxes, unglued from the earth, looking behind and ahead of us.

YSÉ: Behind us is that huge past pushing with an irresistible force, and ahead of us the huge future which inhales us with an irresistible force.

DE CIZ: How bitter it is to be over being young!

MESA: How dangerous it is to begin to be over being alive!

AMALRIC: And how fine it is not to be dead, but to be alive! Alive, you understand!

YSÉ: The morning was so beautiful. Wasn't it Mesa?

MESA: The evening will be still more beautiful. Yesterday did you see everything that came out of the great richness of the sea? [*His eyes closed, he recites as for himself.*] "Green foliage and rose and brown-colored lakes and shafts of red fire in the clear swarming chaos. Oily, color of color, the color of all the colors in the world, the sea, the deep window-glass!" [6]

[32]

[*He opens his eyes again.*] You will see that when they lift up the canvas again. You will see the evening which takes forever to come and which does come at last.

AMALRIC: And I say that the best hour is this one now. I ask for only one thing: to see clearly. Just to see. Distinctly. Things as they are, and not as I want them. To see what I have to do.

DE CIZ: There is no more time to lose.

AMALRIC [*declaiming*]: It is not time that is lacking, but we who do not measure up to it.

MESA: Enough of that! We'll get there!

YSÉ: Amalric, you must have been famous at Pondichéry,[7] as an amateur actor.

AMALRIC: Leave it to me. If my chance passes close by, I'll not miss it.

YSÉ [*leaning on De Ciz's shoulder*]: It is strange however you look at it! The birds and the little fish have a place to put their household, a hedge, a hole under the stump of a willow, but all four of us have been unable to contrive a single place, and here we are lurching about on this moving ship, in the middle of an absurd ocean! Like the fleet! The boat floats and we float! The rest of you are free. But I am not, poor female with my children hanging on to

[33]

my skirt, each one of them with two arms and two legs, and they have mouths too! And I have to live like a boy with these three men who never let me go. My house is this rocking-chair which doesn't belong to me, and eight articles of luggage on the bill of lading. Three steamer trunks, three large trunks and two boxes in the store-room, a suitcase and a hat box. Oh, in God's name! my poor hats!

DE CIZ [*horrified and raising his arms*]: Don't swear like that. It sounds terrible! [*pointing her out to the others.*] You know now that this lady has bad manners!

MESA: We are at an age when it is no longer very reassuring to be free.

AMALRIC: Let's have no bad omens and look at each other's face as if we were playing poker and the cards are dealt. This is important, even before looking at one's own cards. Here we are all participating in the game like four needles, and who knows what kind of wool fate is reserving for all four of us to knit together?

DE CIZ: There is no more time to lose. There is no more time for being difficult. Mesa, please let me ask you one more thing . . .

[*They go off, but not completely out of sight. Ysé is smoking as she stretches out on her rocking-chair. She takes her book. Amalric sits down at some distance from her. As he smokes, he watches her. He soon throws away his cigar. Ysé looks up at him and puts down her book.*]

YSÉ: So, you didn't know we were passengers.

AMALRIC: We had already left shore when I recognized you. A tall woman bolstering herself against the wind!

YSÉ: Did you recognize me right away? Is it true I haven't changed too much in ten years?

AMALRIC: You are the same woman, I swear it! You are even better than the same woman!

YSÉ: Amalric, I heard you were dead.

AMALRIC: What an idea! Me, dead? Not as long as I live!

YSÉ: I was sure we would meet again.

AMALRIC: One look was all I needed. You were the same woman I knew. The same figure. The same form abrupt and black against the sky. Free and erect. There is something about you which makes you seem bold and supple and determined.

YSÉ: Am I still pretty?

[*She looks at him, laughs, blushes, glances at him again. A pause.*]

AMALRIC: I recognized you easily.

YSÉ: I remember now. I was wearing a big coat and a felt hat.

AMALRIC: I said "There she is!" It was you.

YSÉ: I was so pleased. Tell me, in spite of everything, way down deep, we are always happy to get out from wherever we've been living and leave the whole confounded show behind us! Do you agree? When there is no hat and no handkerchief being waved at us?

AMALRIC: Yes!

YSÉ: And no poor little woman somewhere who is snivelling and whose heart is broken? Or some very kind widow? or a small virgin straight as a willow reed and smooth as a whistle? All right! It makes no difference! I was so pleased! [*She laughs.*] Everything was exciting that day! The sky was wicked and ravaged, just as I like it best! And the sea, God! how it lept on you like a Pagan woman! What a sea it was! But here, it's a polished floor we are skating over in utter boredom. And so re-silvered, it is embarrassing, as you said! What a magnificent tarnish we make over it! But you said you like this stagnant water, this water that puts us to sleep . . .

[36]

AMALRIC: I do like it! I like to feel that you bore a hole for yourself in it and go straight ahead. I detest being controlled and tossed and rocked, brushed, beaten, knocked over, as we were, back near Crete—do you remember?—by that crazy wind we could make no head or tail out of. Here, fortunately, everything is finite. Everything is resolved once and for all. The situation is reduced to its first characteristics, as on the days of Creation. The Waters and the Heavens, and my place between them like the hero Izdubar!

YSÉ: A-mal-ric! You didn't always hate to that extent the crazy wind we made no head or tail out of.

[*A silence.*]

AMALRIC: Ysé, why weren't you willing at that moment?

YSÉ: You had no money.

AMALRIC: There was something else.

YSÉ: You seemed too strong to me, too confident, too irritating! Too sure of yourself. It's almost ridiculous, the trust you have in yourself, a kind of religious trust. It is important for me to be needed! You can see that I was able to live without you, Colonel!

[37]

AMALRIC: And what else?

YSÉ: What else? I felt weak beside you. That maddened me.

AMALRIC: Is that the reason you married him?

YSÉ: I love him. I loved him.

AMALRIC: But of the two of you, he isn't the stronger!

YSÉ: When he looks at me in a certain way, I am . . . ashamed! When he looks at me with his big eyes and their long eyelashes—he has the eyes of a woman—with his big black eyes —you can see nothing in his eyes—my heart turns over and I let him have his way. I have tried but I can't hold out.

   [*She laughs silently.*]

AMALRIC: And so that is why you are mad with him. He is in love with you, you know.

YSÉ: He is not in love with me! He loves me in his own way. He loves only himself. You see, I can remember our wedding night. And then all those children I had one after the other. I lost one. Escapes, fears, adventures! All kinds of trouble which creditors bring. You'd have a good laugh if I told you. All the years of my youth are now gone by.

AMALRIC: Ysé, Ysé, do you remember that bright morning when we met? That cold

[38]

bright Sunday, Ysé, at ten o'clock on the ocean? A wild wind was blowing in the full sunlight. It whistled and lashed you. That ferocious Mistral harrowed the water. The whole ocean seemed lifted up, banging, slapping, lashing out in the sun, and scampering away in the storm! It was yesterday, under the moonlight, in the deepest part of night, that finally, as we entered the straits of Sicily, those who woke up and sat upright rubbing off the steam from the port-hole, rediscovered Europe, all wrapped in snow, huge and gray, Europe voiceless, faceless, welcoming them as they slept. And on that clear day of Epiphany, we left Corsica behind us, on our right, all white and radiant like a bride on the morning of chiming bells! You were returning from Egypt then, Ysé, and I was getting back from the end of the world, from the depths of the sea, having drunk my first big draught of life and bringing back in my pocket nothing except a hard fist and fingers able to count. It was then a gust of wind like a slap made all your combs fall out and the mass of your hair swept into my face. The tall young girl turns around and laughs. She looks at me and I look at her.

YSÉ: I remember! You let your beard grow in

[39]

those days. It bristled like a curry-comb. I was strong and happy then, and laughed easily, and behaved myself. I was pretty too! Then life began. The children came. And now you see me sobered and obedient like an old white horse following after the hand which pulls it, and lifting up its four feet one after the other!
[*She imitates a horse, and raises her skirt up to her knees.*]

AMALRIC: I see you can still laugh.

YSÉ: I have been kept in prison, and now I am free. The sea air is in my lungs. Amalric, you shouldn't have believed me so quickly. It was cruel to take my words literally. I was out of my mind on that day. It's strange, I still feel like a little girl. [*She looks down.*] You see, there were no parents to raise me, Amalric! I'm a foreigner. I don't use the right words. I grew up alone, in my own way. Don't judge me too harshly! [*She looks at him again.*] With some-one else it might have been different.

AMALRIC: Those beautiful shining eyes! Now they're full of tears! You're behaving like a fool!
[*A dig in the ribs. They both laugh.*]

YSÉ: And now I'm off on another trip. To where, I don't know.

[40]

AMALRIC: Doesn't your husband have business waiting for him in China?

YSÉ: No, only his luck, in which he has full confidence.

AMALRIC: He's a rubber plant, always ready to encroach and expand. A gluttonous creeper! That gentleman will find his tree, the tree he needs. I have noticed he talks a good deal with our friend Mesa. [*Pause*] Mesa spoke to me about the railroad they are building in the direction of Siam, the telegraph lines in the direction of the Shan States. Do the Shan States mean anything to you?

YSÉ: Nothing at all! We have always managed somehow.

AMALRIC: I like talking with Mesa. He doesn't look at you. Rather than looking directly at you, he seems to be looking at you somewhere else in a mirror. He listens to you from somewhere else—from where your voice resounds. You see every successive thought that comes into his head. I feel sorry for him! He is gruff, stiff and gruff, like those who have in them [*reciting*] "Some fine seed to defend." I think he's a virgin.

YSÉ: Stop making fun of him!

AMALRIC: I'm not making fun of him. Now

you're mad. Why, I like him! I really do! I swear that I like him! Don't be angry!

YSÉ: I respect him, and I want him to respect and like me. Why do you always stay with me and never let me move an inch away? What will people think? A minute ago I saw him looking at us, and I'm sure he saw us yesterday when you kissed me.

AMALRIC: All right! Have it your way. I'll leave you alone.

YSÉ: The other night, seeing him all by himself, I went to him. You remember, the night we had that fellow Léonard sing those miserable café songs. He hadn't stayed with us. Do you remember? I wore my black dress. Don't I look well in it? I went to him and I stayed with him. He called me names, names that no one had ever called me before. What words! A fine greeting, you could say. And I begged his pardon. I cried bitterly like a little girl. Bitterly, or almost. At least that is what I should have done!

AMALRIC: Poor Ysé!

YSÉ: You are right. Poor Ysé!

AMALRIC: Poor Mesa!

YSÉ: Is it true he has an important position in China?

AMALRIC: He was made Customs Commissioner

when still quite young. He speaks every dialect. He is adviser to the viceroys in the south, and in those regions he is more powerful than anyone else. He is a gloomy man, and tired. He has "other plans." He says he is returning for the last time. He has religion, as they say, and that explains the names he called you. Do you understand? That business deal your husband spoke to him about—I don't know what it is—impressed him. I am urging him to be cautious. He is looking for someone to set up lines of communication. It's a very big job. The climate there is far from being good. But your husband, I imagine, is used to the tropics.

YSÉ: He knows a good deal about electricity.

AMALRIC: Well, that's convenient! We can let Mesa and him work it out themselves.

> [*He takes Ysé by the arm and leads her on a few steps as if a band were playing ahead of them. She frees herself.*]

YSÉ: Do you really think, cher monsieur, do you really think, dear Amalric, that I can be led off this easily?

AMALRIC: When I really want to take you, my dear Amazon, I will place my hand on your shoulder, I will take Ysé and hold her and lead her off with this hand of mine, with this hand

[43]

you see here, and which is a big ugly-looking hand.

YSÉ: In that case, I pity you. I don't bring good luck wherever I go.

AMALRIC: After all, Ysé, why wait? These hands of mine give pleasure. You know very well that you will not find anywhere else except with me the pleasure you need, and that I am the man who . . .

YSÉ: So, you are the man! And do you think that the woman has nothing to say?

> [*She stretches out in the rocking-chair. She keeps her eyes on her book. He takes a cigar and moves away. Mesa enters and moves awkwardly toward Ysé. Seeing that she does not look at him, he hesitates.*]

MESA: What are you reading in that book which looks worn and shabby like a love story?

YSÉ: A love story.

MESA [*takes the book from her*]: Page 250. [*He gives it back.*] You were wise to pick off the outside leaves. It is hard to finish. It is always the same story. Death or the mid-wife. One should read in the two directions at the same time.

YSÉ: It's always too long. A love story should be

[44]

as sudden as a flower, for example, or a perfume. You learn about everything, you have it
all, you breathe it all in in one breath, and it
makes you say ah! and that's all! [*a brief sharp
ah!*] A perfume so direct and swift that it
makes you smile, just a bit: ha [*solemn and
aspirate*] and then you're drunk!

MESA: It isn't a flower you smell.

YSÉ: You mean love? I was speaking about a
book. But even love, even—what do you expect? I don't know what it is.

MESA: I wish I did. You're making me say foolish
things. All the same, I can understand. . . .

YSÉ: Understand! Listen to him! You don't need
to *understand*, dear sir, you have to lose consciousness. I am too wicked, I can't! It's an
operation you have. It's the tampon of ether
they clamp over your nose. You remember
about the sleep of Adam. It's in the catechism.
That's the way they made the first woman. A
woman, Mesa, just give it a moment's thought.
One inside the other, all the beings there are to
infinity inside that one creature. You might as
well acknowledge it. She has to die in the arms
of the man who loves her. Do you suppose that
poor innocent creature of the good Lord sus-
pects anything about what is in her and what

is going to come from her? Nothing whatsoever! Every woman is a mother of women and
men!

MESA: What does one ask a woman?

YSÉ: Many things, I should say. To begin with:
the child that wasn't asked for, the little imp
who begins to be born without knowing how
or why.

MESA: I am not interested in children. You didn't
understand what I tried to say to you the other
day. I imagine it is a terrible upheaval. A terrible disturbance of one's substance . . .

> [*He tries to speak, stammers, stutters,
> closes his mouth and looks at her with
> shining eyes and trembling lips. She
> listens to him delightedly, with her
> hands clasped and her tongue between
> her lips. Silence. She begins to laugh.*]

YSÉ: Speak, professor, I am listening. There is no
reason for you to get angry.

MESA: Quite simply, everything in him demands
everything in the woman. That is what I meant.
Go ahead and laugh. There's no point in laughing without a good reason. I wasn't speaking
about a child. That little imp, as you call him,
in being born, we don't know how, profits
from that moment we take from eternity. But

[46]

love is only a form of low comedy badly acted
by the man and the woman. Questions aren't
asked. Yes, that is what I meant. [*shouting*]
Questions aren't asked. Do you understand
me?

YSÉ [*very demure*]: Sometimes the play is amusing.

MESA: Perhaps. I have no sense of humor.

YSÉ: But you speak better than my book does,
when you want to. How your eyes sparkle,
professor, when you are made to speak philo-
sophically! You have beautiful gray eyes. I
love to watch you listen when you are boiling
with anger. I love to hear you speak, even when
I don't follow you. What a queer thing a soul
is! Be my professor! Don't be afraid! I am un-
educated. I'm stupid. Don't judge me harshly.
I am not as bad as you think, but I don't think
before speaking. I never had a teacher. No one
ever spoke to me as you did, the other evening.
I know that you are right. I am a bad woman.

MESA: I have no right to judge you.

YSÉ: Stay here, don't go away.

MESA: I don't want to go away.

YSÉ: You see, I don't know what you are thinking. Here we are, the two of us. You and I, and
how sad it is! Listen! As time passes between

us, it makes a tiny crackling sound. Between us there is such suspense that just the speck of a bad thought upsets it. Poor Mesa! you seem so unhappy. Mesa! Don't think me full of joy.

MESA: I am not unhappy.

YSÉ: Someone should take care of you. I was told you have stopped eating. Why that fierce look?

MESA: I am not unhappy. And I have nothing to say to you. Those phrases are stupid: "Someone told me," "I was told" . . . Go talk with Amalric. You're not my mother and you don't have to flirt with me. If I have a problem, it's my own business. If something is worrying me, I'll keep it to myself.

YSÉ: Don't lose your temper.

MESA: You'd like to make me talk. It would amuse you to see me go limping and blubbering about here. How well you know that those fat devils called men like nothing better than to talk and lie and bare their noble hearts! If you knew how I suffered! If you knew how handsome I am! I have nothing to say to you. You are happy, aren't you? That should be enough.

YSÉ: Do you really believe I am happy?

MESA: You must be. You should be.

YSÉ: Should I? If I want that happiness, whatever it is you call happiness, I'll have to become

[48]

someone else! Woe to me if I am not prepared to shake it from my head like a beautiful coiffure when you let it down!

MESA: Keep that forage of hair tightly pressed in place. And let your tender child as he holds his tender mother in his arms lovingly smooth out near her tiny ear the untidy lock that is hanging down. Are you laughing? Are you blushing? Try to deny you are happy.

YSÉ: Don't upbraid me.

MESA: I like to watch you. You are beautiful.

YSÉ: Do you really think so? I am glad of that.

MESA: It frightens me to see you so beautiful and young and animated, with this fellow you have for a husband and who knows the country where you are going.

YSÉ: Amalric said the same thing to me. Don't despair! We are going to stay for a while in Hong-Kong. For the time being. [*Silence*] It's where you live, I believe. Well, aren't you pleased?

MESA: I am not going back to China for very long. Just the time needed to put my affairs in order.

YSÉ: One year, perhaps? Two years?

MESA: I guess so, approximately.

YSÉ: And after that?

MESA: After that, nothing!

YSÉ: A year, perhaps, two years more or less, and after that, nothing?

MESA: Yes, after that, nothing! What difference does it make to you? Your life is organized! I am a hound dog. You know, one of those pariah dogs. But my life is no concern of yours. Everyone loves you.

YSÉ: Are you angry at that?

MESA: Live your own life, your own offensive life! I have decided to have nothing. I have left mankind.

YSÉ: Just listen to him! He says he has left mankind! Why, you're taking the whole collection with you!

MESA: Go ahead and laugh! You are beautiful and happy, and I am morbid and alone . . . One of those miserable hound dogs . . . And I want nothing whatsoever! [*a kind of hiccup*] What could you ever do with me? What is there between you and me?

[*Eleven A.M. Six bells.*]

YSÉ: Mesa, I am Ysé.

MESA: It's too late. Everything is over. Why did you come to talk with me again?

YSÉ: Because I found you.

MESA: I tell you that everything is over! I wasn't

[50]

expecting you. I had made careful plans to re-
tire, to withdraw from mankind, yes, from all
of mankind. Why not? I had actually accomplished it. Why did you come to talk with me
again? Why did you come to upset me?

YSÉ: Women are created just for that reason.

MESA: I was wrong to talk with you and . . .
become sociable with you and feel no distrust,
as with a lovely child whose face you like to
see because it is beautiful. Here the child is a
woman, that's the crazy part of it. We laugh
when she laughs. What role is there for me to
play with you, or you with me? I tell you
everything is over! Is this you? No, not any
more you than someone else. What is there to
expect? What is there to understand in a
woman? And after all, what does she have that
she can give you? Whatever she asks of you,
you would have to give yourself completely to
her. There is absolutely no way, and what
would be the use of it? There is no way by
which I can give you my soul, Ysé! That is
why I turned in another direction. Now tell me
why you came to upset me? Why you came to
seek me out again? It was [*swallowing his
saliva*] cruel. Why did I ever meet you? And
now you turn toward me your lovely face and

[51]

fix your attention on me. It is too late. You
know how impossible it is. And I know that
you don't love me. In the first place, you are
married, and in the second place I know that
you are attracted [*pause*] to that other man
Amalric. But why do I say this and what difference does it make? Do whatever you want. We
shall soon be separated. At least, what I have
belongs to me.

YSÉ: What is it you fear in me since I represent
the impossible? Are you afraid of me? Raise
your eyes and look at me who am looking at
you with my impossible face.

MESA: I know that you are not attracted to me.

YSÉ: That is not the point, but I don't understand
who you are, or what you want, or what I have
to be, or how I have to act with you. You are
strange. Don't make a face. That's ugly. Yes, I
think you are right. You are not a man made
for a woman, a man in whom she would feel
happy and secure.

MESA: That is true. I must be alone.

YSÉ: It will be better for us to land and not be
together any more.

[*Pause.*]

MESA: Why has all this happened? And why
should I have met you on this boat, at this mo-

ment when my strength is low because of the blood I lost? Do you believe in God?

YSÉ: I don't know. I never thought of it.

MESA: But you believe in yourself and you have a deep conviction that you are beautiful. There is no doubt of that!

YSÉ: It is not my fault if I am beautiful.

MESA: At least with you, a man knows who you are and with whom he is dealing, but imagine someone with you—and this sounds ridiculous —[*he speaks mysteriously, close to her ear*] forever! [*he moves off and looks at her attentively*] Another person in you and whom you have to tolerate. [*Facing the public.*] He lives and I live. He thinks and I weigh His thought in my heart. It was He who made my eyes. Couldn't I at least see Him? It was He who made my heart and I can't get rid of Him. [*He turns his back to her.*] You don't understand. But it is not a question of understanding. I am speaking about eyes which just in looking at you make you comprehensible. [*Facing the public.*] The torment of feeling oneself studied, spelled out by someone who never comes to the end of what He is doing. He never leaves me for a minute's peace! I fled to this extreme end of the earth, away from the old house on

[53]

the farm with its piles of manure. How I loved all things visible! Oh! I had so many things to ask them and they had so many things to tell me. I wanted to know everything so that everything about me would be known. What a pity that I was needed! Even in China there was someone who sought me out. I am like a debtor who is hard pressed and who doesn't know what he owes. . . .

YSÉ: Is that when you went back to France?

MESA: What could I do? Where was my mistake? Is it fair to be coerced for an obligation I don't recognize? Well, here I am! Pay yourself. You take what you need!

YSÉ: Were you rejected?

MESA: I wasn't rejected. It was like standing before someone who looked at me and said nothing. Not a word. Things aren't going well in China. They are sending me back here for a while.

YSÉ: Learn how to endure time.

MESA: What else have I done these last five years? In the midst of men I have lived in total solitude. I didn't find my place in harmony with them! I am of no usefulness, I have nothing to give or receive. So, let the giver of funds take back his money. I am delighted to

give it back to Him. "No . . ." I left and I
must return to the same place. Nothing has
been accomplished. Once there was in me the
force of a great hope. It is no longer there. And
now with my former life, I am sent back naked
and dry, with the sole order to begin over again
my former life. Almighty God, I am separated
from life, with no expectation except You
alone who do not want me, and my heart is
pierced [*he turns toward Ysé*] and my strength
is false. Here I am chattering with you. I wonder how this concerns you or interests you.

YSÉ: It does concern me. I see your thoughts in
a blurred way like sparrows near a haystack
when you clap your hands, mounting all together to your lips and eyes.

MESA: You do not understand me.

YSÉ: I understand that you are unhappy.

MESA: At least that belongs to me.

YSÉ: Yes, that is so. Wouldn't it be better if I
belonged to you?

[*Pause.*]

MESA: That is impossible.

YSÉ: Of course it is impossible.

MESA: Let me look at you, since I can't have you.

YSÉ: Poor Mesa! It is strange, but I have never
seen you. I like all of your features, but no one

[55]

certainly would think of calling you handsome. Perhaps it is because you aren't tall enough. No, you aren't good-looking at all.

MESA: Tell me, Ysé, what difference does that make? Soon we shall be separated. It is of no consequence. Suppose that we were both free. Would you [*speaks close to her ear inaudibly*] consent to marry me?

YSÉ: No, Mesa.

MESA: Ysé. I know that you are Ysé.

YSÉ: That is true. Why did I speak the way I did just now? I don't know. I don't know what came over me all of a sudden. Something very new forced me to speak. The words were hardly out and I was shocked. Do you always know what you are saying?

MESA: I know that you don't love me.

YSÉ [*clapping her hands*]: Yes, that is what surprised me. That is what I learned in a flash. It is unbelievable, but it's true! Yes, on my word, it is true! I am the woman you would have loved.

MESA: Let me look at you. How ironic it is to have you here with me! If I raise my hand, [*He slightly raises it but does not touch her.*] I can touch you, and if I speak, you will answer me and you will hear what I say.

[56]

YSÉ: I didn't expect this! I wasn't paying attention to you. I respect you. I wasn't a flirt with you. You can't say I was . . . That isn't a pleasant thought!

MESA: Why is it now that I have met you? Oh! I was made for happiness! It is a hard thing to keep all of one's heart. It is hard not to be loved. It is hard to be alone. It is hard to wait! And endure and wait and still wait! And here I am at this time of noon when I see so clearly what is very near, so near that I can see nothing else. And behold! you are here! How close the present seems! What is immediate is close at hand like something having the force of necessity! My strength has gone. Oh God! I . . . I cannot wait any longer!

YSÉ: No, no, you mustn't love me, Mesa. It would not be right. You know that I am weak. You must be the Mesa I need, who is rude and stupid and kind, who spoke to me a few nights ago. Who will there be for me to respect and love, if you love me? No, Mesa, you must not love me. I only wanted to talk and tease you a bit. I thought I was stronger than you in a certain way. Tell me, are you surprised when I swear? Now I am the one who is stupid, and who can't talk, who is reduced to silence and

[57]

who listens! You know that I am weak and if
you speak to me in a certain way, you don't
need to raise your voice. But if you call me by
my name, by your name, by a name you know
and I don't, when I hear it there is a woman in
me who will not be able to keep from answering you. She would not be right for you, she
would be deadly. I feel there are deadly things
all about me! This is no game with you. I don't
want to give all of myself. And I don't want to
die. I am young and death is not beautiful, it is
life that seems beautiful to me. On this boat,
life has gone to my head. That is why everything must be over between us. All has been
said, Mesa. All is over between us. Let's agree
not to fall in love. Say after me that you will
not love me. Ysé, I will not love you.

MESA: "Ysé, I will not love you."

YSÉ: "Ysé, I will not love you."

[*She listens, her eyes closed.*]

MESA: I will not love you.

YSÉ: Once again let me hear it.

[*She places her ear near his mouth.*]

MESA [*with his lips only*]: I will not love you.

AMALRIC [*Noisily comes up from the lower deck
    with a tray bearing drinks.*]: Monsieur, Ma-
    dame, pardon me, excuse me for disturbing

[58]

you. Mesa is needed for the masked ball tonight. The singer from Saigon says she can't
do without him. She wants his advice. She is
wearing a corset and her back is attracting attention. There are more unpleasant things to
look at than a woman's back. It is thick velvet
[*a greedy gesture with his finger*]. Thick white
velvet. The only thing prettier was the ox they
were skinning yesterday on the deck. You
should have seen it. It was iridescent and had
the lustre of pearls. When I think of what you
can have under your skin! Well, Mesa, my
little parish priest, now you're hearing the con-
fessions of pretty women. There are more unpleasant things to do than hearing the confes-
sions of pretty women.

YSÉ: He's giving me a lecture. It is refreshing to
be lectured at from time to time. You remember, he is my professor!

AMALRIC: More likely you are his professor.

YSÉ: You can learn so much from him. He
knows women. In a way, he's here to give
advice. He is one of those men always ready to
offer his life and who would give it to you on
the condition that he would be rid of you. An
extreme type, crotchety, no moderation. Always giving more than he needs to. It's true

[59]

now, what I'm saying. That's why I like little Mesa. It's the way I am myself.

MESA: I realize that. It is good to be close to a woman. It is like being seated in the shade. I like to hear her speak with her great wisdom, and tell me things that are hard and malicious and practical and contemptibly true, as only women can say them. It does me good.

AMALRIC: Things that your husband hears. The good fellow smiles and you feel that he is about to say something, but he says nothing. He is thinking of what can be made out of the situation.

YSÉ: Poor boy!

AMALRIC: Can it be possible that you're in love with him?

YSÉ: I'm in love with him. And I'm the man. I love him as you love a woman.

[*She laughs loudly.*]

MESA [*wincing*]: You mustn't laugh that way.

YSÉ: It's all right for me to, professor. I am not a French woman.

[*She laughs.*]

AMALRIC: Look at the way he winces when you laugh. It gets on his nerves. It irritates him, but he loves it. I too at night sometimes remember your laugh and then I begin to curse.

YSÉ: I like a man who is a man all by himself and who has a strong back bone.

AMALRIC: A strong back bone? That's me. The types women admire the most are the negro and the truckdriver. Both types are in me: negro and truckdriver!

MESA: I like the stevedores on this ship, when they come up from down below in the evening, and their white teeth pray in this Arabian desert of an ocean. When you've dug all day in the coal-dust, nourishing the yellow Sultan, how much dignity can you have when you soberly grab your mug of water. Those of us who are white are talkative, cynical, petticoated, wearing breeches, heavy-drinkers, pork-eaters!

AMALRIC: We're not at our best in this boat promiscuity.

MESA: How disgusting it is to sit down at the same table with the rest of the herd of hairless animals whose cleanliness smells bad!

YSÉ: What a character! He amuses me, he is so neatly organized. It is comical to see all of him walk about, speak, sit down, turn around [*she looks at Mesa*], put a hand in the pocket of his pants. [*He withdraws it.*] You want to laugh at him. And you know that a boat, with all its

[61]

compartments, with all these doors you can open and close, is a handsome jewel. It's like the box of a naturalist with his collection. All the species together. It is amusing to see how the passengers come close and recognize one another, with the kinds of antennae they use to feel a face, and to notice how they are costumed, combed, what shoes and ties they have on, the book they hold in their hand, their nails, the shape of their ears, the tip of their tongue showing between thin lips like a fat almond. Just one of their hands opening and moving, and busy with its small fingers, how easy to understand what it is saying!

MESA: They bore me.

YSÉ: What do they think of you?

MESA: I don't know. I am not concerned with them. I don't worry about other people.

YSÉ: Mesa! Mesa!

MESA: But it's true. Does this mean that I think only of myself?

> [*Ysé and Amalric laugh and look at one another.*]

YSÉ: Are you discovering this for the first time? Try to deny that women are useful. It's a comfortable feeling just to be concerned with oneself. One never tires of looking at oneself, be-

cause one is so infinitely nice. I know people
who are always ready to offer themselves, but
to give oneself for good is something quite
different. What is your opinion, Mesa?

MESA: It's true.

YSÉ: Let the women teach you one thing, professor. A woman is more in the way than you
think. A woman all for yourself, whom you
need, day in and day out, and not any other
woman. She gives herself to you, and does the
fine gentleman give himself to her?

AMALRIC: All this is too subtle for me. God!
what if a man had to worry frantically all the
time over his wife, to learn whether he has
estimated accurately the affection which Ger-
maine or Petronille deserves, by checking the
state of her heart. What a job! Sentiment is
housekeeping for women, like those boxes
where they put away piles of thread and ribbon
and buttons and corset ribs. The disgusting
part is that they're sick all the time. But she's
in the house, she's always there. You have to
put up with her as best you can. And if she
weren't there, you'd miss her. It's nice to have
her there from time to time. What do you say
to that, my boy? Am I right or wrong?

YSÉ: Amalric . . . what did our friend, the

[63]

leather salesman, call you? Amalric, you're a rabbit!

[*She laughs.*]

AMALRIC: And I must tell you, dear Madame, not to get too aroused over Mesa. I know him better than you do. We play cards together every day. He has committed too few dishonest actions in his life. Just wait for the first opportunity to come along. Here is your husband. Always distinguished and silent, an aristocrat!

[*Enter De Ciz.*]

AMALRIC [*calling him*]: Félicien, what do you know! We're all going to become rich!

DE CIZ: Amen!

AMALRIC: No doubt about it! In the first place, don't we all need money? So! [*He grabs hold of him and shakes him.*] Ask the lady here. And Mesa who is like a man without pockets. I'm not mentioning you and me. I tell you I smell fortune in the air. I can sniff it. I'm filling up my money box. [*With a roar.*] I know all about such things. I recognize the smell. It's something blowing in your face. I feel it. My heart is growing bigger. We have gone beyond a certain line. I recognize the old East. For me

[64]

it is what the department store of the Louvre is for the lady from a distant province, a place crammed with cloth and soap. India is just ahead of us. Don't you hear it? It's so crowded that you hear the flickering of millions of eyelids. What luck not to be in France! And we won't go back! All that fodder was tasteless and watery. What filth in that endless stretch of green.[8] And no sun except a pale water-heater! A kind of sick Pierrot who stuck his tongue out at you through a round window.

DE CIZ: We have just passed Suez.

AMALRIC: We'll never pass it again. Good! We'll never go back. Hurrah! But we'll all be dead next year, my chicks. All of us dead and buried next year, my little friends. Hurrah!

YSÉ: What a beautiful prayer!

AMALRIC [*serves drinks to everyone. Throughout the rest of the act he keeps filling the glasses.*]: In any case, we must all become rich, and if we don't, it's our own fault. Now it's in our power. I want to make a huge pile. I recognize the East I love. "I'm wild and wooly and full of fleas!" [9] In the East, the sun comes from the sun, thank God! Green is really green, and the heat can easily kill you, and dammit, when there's red, everything is red! You've seen a tiger in the circus? Well, a man is like a tiger in the midst of weaker animals! Of course, in place of disgusting commerce, it would be better to make your entrance with the saber in your fist, and strike terror [*clowning*] in the old cities reeking with human flesh, determined to go home with four casks for yourself filled with jewels, and here and there a few heathen ears and fingers cut off from the hands of ladies and young girls, or perish with honor in the midst of your companions. That would be better than sweating in your pyjamas before your ledger-book.

YSÉ: Save the pearls for me, please!

AMALRIC: Well, anyway, say a prayer that I will find workers for my rubber plantation. Then you'll see the price I'll sell it for! Time brings no change. It's always the same sun. It's always India, trained by the two monsoons, the old bitter Pagan! The tenth degree for a sailor at the spot when he cuts the 60th. It is the same for Belgium, Labrador and 25th Street, New York. And still more! The earth is dull and solid, but the helmsman feels the ways of this land of water and how it moves. It always stays the same. Tell me, do you know where we are?

Do you understand business methods? Now listen, I am going to teach you economics.

MESA: You're drunk, Amalric!

DE CIZ: Never as drunk as he would like us to believe he is. He's a seasoned traveler. Look at his small eye wink.

AMALRIC: On the left, Babylon with all of its commerce and the rivers coming down from Armenia. On the right the equator and Africa. Well, now do you see the business possibilities? The big boats in the monsoon of the north, sailing from Sheba, sailing from the ports of Solomon, sailing from Arabia and India, sailing from the mouth of the Two Rivers, boats loaded with iron and fabrics, and enough chains and handcuffs for the slaves, sailing toward Cimbabasia and the Oval Cities.[10] And returning into the monsoon of the south with a pocket-full of the tribe of Ham, negroes, negresses, nigger boys shouting, eating, dancing, singing, crying, shitting, pissing. And on some mornings you'll see the black buttocks of the large motionless boat, surrounded by chicken feathers and banana skins on the sea spitting out flying fish. All that would be useful for rubber.

[67]

YSÉ [*stretches out on the rocking-chair*]: Now we have really passed Suez.

MESA: We shall never pass it again.

[*Pause.*]

AMALRIC: In a few minutes it will be noon.

MESA: We are going to hear the siren. What a queer name that is! Siren!

YSÉ: There is no more sky, and no more sea. There is nothing left but the void, and in the middle, striking terror, is that species of a fossil animal which is going to begin to bray!

MESA: A cry in this desert of fire!

YSÉ: The brontosaur is going to begin to bray.

DE CIZ: Sss! Look here! [*He opens the canvas just a bit.*]

YSÉ: For God's sake, don't open the canvas!

AMALRIC: I'm blinded as if a rifle went off in my face. That's much more than just the sun.

DE CIZ: It's as strong as lightning. We would be burnt up and crumble to bits in that furnace.

AMALRIC: You feel visible in a stark kind of way, like a louse held between two pieces of glass.

MESA [*near the crack of the tarpaulin*]: It is beautiful and hard. The sea with its dazzling back is like a cow thrown to the ground that is being branded with a red-hot iron. And her

[68]

lover, as they say, well, the sculpturing you see in museums, Baal, this time isn't her lover, he's the executioner sacrificing her. They're not kisses she feels any more, it's the knife in her bowels. And facing him, she returns blow for blow. Formless, colorless, pure, absolute, large, thundering. Struck by the light, she can't reflect anything else.

YSÉ [*yawning*]: It's hot! How many days more before we reach the fire of Minnicoi?

MESA: I remember that small dim light on the water.

DE CIZ: Amalric, do you know how many days there are?

AMALRIC: No! And I don't even know how many days there have been since we left.

MESA: The days are so much alike that you might say they make only one long black and white day.

AMALRIC: I like this huge motionless day. I'm very comfortable here. I love this huge shadowless hour. I exist. I am living. I am not sweating, I smoke my cigar, I am content.

YSÉ: Hear that contented man! And you, Mesa, are you content too? I am not.

[*She laughs, but the solemn silence which is settling down is stronger.*]

MESA: There is no place where we could stop if we wanted to.

DE CIZ [*pulling out his watch*]: Be quiet! The hour is going to sound. . . .

[*Long pause. Eight bells.*]

AMALRIC: Eight bells.

MESA [*raising his finger*]: Noon.

[*Pause. The siren sounds at great length. Another pause during which the four actors resume their motionless position they had at the beginning.*]

ACT II

The cemetery (so called) of Hong-Kong: Happy Valley. A large empty Chinese tomb (style of Fou tcheou) in the form of Omega, surrounded by bamboo. The form of the Ω and the opening in a hemicycle bordered with bamboo give the impression of a trap. In the distance low small fires are visible. On the ground, inscriptions of empty tombs in disorderly piles. Among them is a cross. A pile of swept leaves. A wheelbarrow. A broom. The dark close sky of a southern monsoon which is beginning. A sun eclipse is announced. A distant noise of gongs and firecrackers which starts up from time to time throughout the act, while the eclipse advances.

MESA [*enters from up stage and comes to stand at the center of the tomb. On the altar in front of the double Chinese character a piece of broken marble on which is written in large letters the name:* SMITH.]: This is the place. There can be no possible mistake. One empty Chinese tomb remaining from the first cemetery, which the white man came and took possession of. Hard luck for the first occupants. Each one has his turn. I wonder what those small lights flaring up on the ground mean. I don't much care. But I rather like the idea of those small lights burning. Parsees, I imagine. [*He is now in the center of the tomb, between the two claws of the Omega which bend back.*] This is the place. The dignity of these Chinese tombs can't be denied. This kind of Omega is like arms coming to get you and then holding you warmly. In the open air. There is no way of escaping if you want to. SMITH. There it is. You come to take a drink with Mr. Tchang lao Yé and all he says back to you is SMITH. A man who is a pretext for existence found only those five letters. SMITH. Original! Was it worth the trouble to leave Birmingham or Leeds to mingle Smith with all the refuse of other personalities which the cemetery keeper found convenient to pile up in this corner while waiting for the broom and wheelbarrow. [*He examines the outside of the tomb and kicks against the cross which he carefully places in the wheelbarrow.*] "At least I am suffering. At least I am very unhappy." Now I'm beginning to talk to myself! The taste of

[74]

my stomach is in my mouth. [*Nauseated grimace.*] "Plunkett." [*He stands for a moment absent-mindedly, and then vigorously recovers.*] So it is! Plunkett! "Mary Bensusan, deceased at the age of six months." How interesting all this is! Why, that old Cockney. Jones A. G. Baxter, insurance agent. Jehosaphat's telephone directory. Cohn, stock broker. *Donec immutatio mea veniat.* I can see it all now. The sailor of 1859, killed with a jungle bullet or dead from Cantonese small-pox, the old bachelor dying from *delirium tremens* and syphilis. *Mourned for by all his friends,* and the poor infants dying in the suffocating heat of July, like fish asphyxiated in a bowl where the water hasn't been changed. No benediction was said over all this. But she said she would meet me here. There's no denying it, I am caught! You begin to have a kind of heart which beats where the soul is. My soul has suddenly given out. A fatal poisoned sweetness. [*He spits.*] Outside a sky blocked from view, lighted upside down by a pale day, a kind of monsoon weather like an autoclave kettle, and inside . . . [*A moment's silence. Shakes himself.*] What is inside? Poison. A poison that takes away your feelings. A kind of paralysis

[75]

overcoming you! "All is finished." [*Pause*]
Inside, my soul is like a gold piece in the fingers
of a gambler. Heads or tails. No, not gold.
Lead. I'm going to leave. It will be quite a jolt
for that lady to find no one here. [*Humming.*]
Yes, I think it will be quite a jolt for that
la-a-dy . . .

> [*He leaves at the side. De Ciz and Ysé
> enter from the left, from the stairway
> going down.*]

DE CIZ: Please excuse me, my dear. I am sorry,
but I have to leave you here. I have to meet
someone. Go ahead and say that I don't know
how to manage things. How many days have
we been here? Well, the business deal is already
beginning to shape up. Just let me take care of
it. You are always one to doubt me. I have
to speak to someone near here for my friend
Ah Fat. You know him. He's that fat China-
man at the junk harbor. I'm dining with him
tonight. A few final arrangements to fix before
I leave for Swatow.

YSÉ: Is it dangerous?

DE CIZ [*gesture of impatience*]: I don't think so.
But I don't really know. Do you think that I'm
afraid? It's an honest little business deal full
of "goodness" and "sincerity."

[76]

[*With his finger he traces Chinese characters in the air.*]

YSÉ: You do learn languages fast.

DE CIZ: I already know many characters. Once upon a time I collected document stamps.

YSÉ: I know how intelligent you are, Félicien. If you wanted, you could be a business man like everyone else. What makes you behave like a dishonest child?

DE CIZ: Dishonest! It is the circumstances that are dishonest. You'll see if I'm a child. There's no one my equal to relieve people of the desire they had, without realizing it, to do me a good turn. It would be a shock for me to learn that there is opium and guns in the caskets of those good coolies from Pinay or Singapour that are being brought back into the country. You must know that they're trying to put a nice little republic on its feet. It's great fun. It's the American Constitution, blessed by the Three-Genii of the Celestial Banner, with the levying of a few indirect taxes, of course. What would my uncle the marquis say, if he knew that I was helping to found a republic? What can I say, my dear? One has to live. A strange profession for an educated man. What do you think of the deal?

[77]

YSÉ: What do you expect me to think? You'd do well to keep it all to yourself.

DE CIZ: You can never tell. You bait the line to catch small fish. What I said to Mesa the other night wasn't enough to put him on his guard.

YSÉ: I'm not sure.

DE CIZ: It makes no difference. He's a friend. A real friend. It's strange how close I feel to him.

YSÉ: Let's use him then! For as much as he's worth!

DE CIZ: There is a ruthlessness in you I have never gotten used to. It's that determination of yours to insist and exaggerate and dot all the "i's." We should keep a certain lightness about all we do. You remember that children's game when they pretend they have no weight. I like Mesa. I'm really glad he can be of service to me. And besides, he has no real responsibility in the matter.

YSÉ: When did you say you are coming back?

DE CIZ [*at one gulp*]: In a month, two weeks, six weeks. I don't know exactly.

YSÉ: You've never been exact about anything.

DE CIZ: The hotel is perfectly comfortable. And you are used to hotels. Mesa will keep you company.

[78]

YSÉ: Don't go.

    [*Her eyes are lowered.*]

DE CIZ: But I've told you I have to. I haven't a cent left. It's imperative.

YSÉ: Don't go. [*Pause.*]

DE CIZ [*smooth-tongued*]: I have to, Madame Ysé.

YSÉ: Don't leave me alone.

DE CIZ: Alone? There's no danger of that.

YSÉ: I repeat, you shouldn't leave me alone here.

DE CIZ: And I repeat that you have to be reasonable.

YSÉ: I am only a woman, and I am afraid. After all, whatever you are, it is you who are responsible for me. I am afraid. I am! There are terrible things lurking about. I am afraid of this stifling country I don't know. You are leaving me alone just after coming here. I'm still dizzy from the pitching of that boat.

DE CIZ: Bless my soul! Is it you saying you're afraid?

YSÉ: Take me with you.

DE CIZ: You can't leave the children.

YSÉ: You're worried about your children, but not at all about me.

DE CIZ: It's always "me," "me," "me."

YSÉ: I beg you not to go off and leave me alone. You accused me of being proud, of never wanting to say anything or ask for anything. Well, that's over! I'm humiliating myself. Don't leave me. Don't leave me alone.

DE CIZ [*cajoling*]: So, at last, the lady needs someone. She needs her good kind husband. It's proud Ysé asking like a little child not to be left alone!

YSÉ: Don't be too sure of me.

DE CIZ: You belong to me. Did you want to marry me? Well, whether you liked it or not, it was I who took you and won you after others had failed.

[*He kisses her shoulder.*]

YSÉ: Don't be too scornful of me. Don't be too sure of me. As of a woman you hold by caressing her. Haven't I stayed ten years with you? For ten years I've looked at you. Front and back and side and underneath and above, and now I've reached an opinion. Yes, a kind of opinion, in my own terms, about you. Haven't you had your full payment from me? Didn't you have all your children from me? Let me ask: do you know me? Do you know who I am? A man doesn't know his wife any more than he knows his mother. God! ten years! To think that now I'm thirty, and my youth is over, and what I could give you is over. I've

[80]

given it all. Don't leave me alone now when something is just over. Don't be away.

DE CIZ: I know you better than you know yourself. You are proud, Ysé, and with me! I know you too well to believe that you wanted to harm our relationship.

YSÉ: I am not sure. A temptation is growing in me. I am no longer that young girl you took. You didn't spare me very much. I am no longer intact. Do you think that I am useful only for producing children? Is my beauty for no possible use? If any man had me, I would want to keep him from having anything else. If I am his, isn't that enough? I haven't given you the complete self that I am. There is a certain death that I can give. But I knew that you were not serious. Fundamentally not serious.

DE CIZ: Am I bad? Did I ever forbid your doing anything?

YSÉ: I wish you had. I wish you had kept me from myself. I am a woman, after all. A woman isn't that complicated. What does she want? Something beyond security, like a fly after honey in the hive that is clean and shut? But not that terrible freedom! I gave myself. And I wanted to believe that I would be at peace, that I was insured, that there was always someone with me, to lead me, a man for whatever idea I might have, someone who would see to it he was stronger than me. And the pain you caused would not matter provided I felt you held me and I was serving you. But is there anyone who knows you, who has faith in you, who will find in you something to understand and love? You run away, you are never present. You are like a weak affectionate child, but not in the least affectionate, capricious, secretive, full of lies, dishonest. And your eyes reveal nothing. Don't go ahead with this trip. Don't be away from me in the middle of my life!

DE CIZ: All this talk for a few days absence!

YSÉ: What if it is the time when a separation is all that is needed? A knife is a narrow blade but the two halves of the fruit it cuts will never be rejoined. It's possible that I might die, for example, as soon as you leave. [*Sound of gong in distance.*] Listen to me. [*very low*] I am afraid of dying. Why did you bring me here? Look at this mournful place where we are. It is warm here and I am cold.

DE CIZ: But it was you who thought this place attractive, and insisted on showing it to me.

YSÉ [*almost to herself*]: It is a terrible thing to

[82]

die and to be dead. [*She reads the inscription on the tomb.*] SMITH.

DE CIZ: You are not going to die. Why are you always talking about death? You have a little temperature, perhaps. Take some quinine when you go back to the hotel. There is no danger. I shall be back soon. We shall soon have money, a good deal of money, and we shall go back to France. You remember how beautiful France is. It is the only country I love. We'll go back to France, or somewhere else. Go on talking until doomsday. I know that you love me. I know it, sweetheart. I know it, *bonita!*

YSÉ: And you want to leave?

DE CIZ: I have to. I am not free. Ah Fat has loaned me money.

YSÉ: You can go. I have nothing else to say. It's all right.

DE CIZ: And you're not mad with me?

YSÉ: Not in the least. I am not mad at you.
            [*Pause.*]

DE CIZ: Ysé! I've thought about the advice you gave me. You are right, in a way. Those two things that Mesa suggested.

YSÉ: Yes?

DE CIZ: There isn't much future if we stay here.

YSÉ: But this place is secure.

[83]

DE CIZ: Secure! That's the one word you keep using. You have never understood me. I need an initiative. I need money that I can earn. It intoxicates me. It's true that money doesn't particularly like me, but you know what a fondness I have for it. I'm not afraid of taking risks. But I couldn't at the beginning take you to this other place.

YSÉ: That's why you shouldn't go.

DE CIZ: It's a pity. It will take just a few years. My position will be made, and I will be in control.

YSÉ: How can one side with you! You keep changing your mind.

DE CIZ: Don't be hard on me. I'll soon be gone. Goodby, sweetheart.

YSÉ: Goodby, Félicien. After all, you were good to me.

DE CIZ: No tears, sweetheart. Goodby, *bonita!* I am not leaving you alone. I am glad that Mesa is here to keep you company.

> [*He kisses her hand and goes off upstage. Ysé watches him as he slowly disappears.*]

YSÉ [*looking in another direction*]: I can't see him. And I won't wait for him. He may not have been able to come. It's better that way.

[*Ysé is stage left. Mesa appears stage right. Silence.*]

YSÉ: My husband has just left. He wouldn't give up that trip.

MESA [*speaking with difficulty*]: How are you?

YSÉ: Oh! I'm fine! My appetite's good! [*She laughs, a bit strained.*] I'm like a good soldier who is going to fight. It's curious, I haven't yet got my ground legs. I veer to the side, and bend over. And then I give a kick, as in bed when you don't want to sleep. Do you feel this way? On a boat you never feel right when you stand erect, because nothing is straight. You don't stand, you catch hold as if you were on a floor that breathes.

MESA: Did you speak to him?

YSÉ: I asked him not to go, not to leave me here alone. He wouldn't listen to me. He said no.

MESA: I too did what I could. How can he leave you this way? I made suggestions to him. He prefers his own intrigues. He enjoys them. He imagines he is tricking me. On all sides you can hear talk of revolution.

YSÉ: Is anything about to break?

MESA: The end of the world is always imminent.

[*Gong and firecrackers.*]

YSÉ: Listen!

MESA: Didn't you read the paper? There is an eclipse of the sun. So it must be helped along. The sun mustn't be devoured that easily by an evil dragon. So, let's play misty music and shoot off firecrackers.

YSÉ: They can't believe in all that.

MESA: Of course they don't believe in it, but they pretend to. And I too at times pretend. Did I say imminent? Not really imminent, but the old machine is breaking down. It's a crazy feeling that everything around here, the whole kit and kaboodle, is going to fall on your head. When did you say he's going to leave?

YSÉ: Tomorrow.

MESA: And how long will he be away, if I have the right to ask you?

YSÉ: One month. And you realize you must leave me alone. You mustn't come to see me.

MESA: Of course.

[*He comes close to her almost touching her from behind, as if instinctively.*]

YSÉ: There is someone behind me who would like to go away and who cannot. [*From behind he raises trembling hands over her.*] God drove you away, but I won't.

MESA: It's over. I have found you.

[*His trembling hands without touching*

[86]

her go over all her body. Gradually they take on more and more fervent possession of her.]

YSÉ: I am not moving away. Someone is behind me whom I can't see and who has come to me from I don't know where.

MESA: Oh Ysé! What I am doing is forbidden.

YSÉ: Are you sure? I didn't know that I was forbidden.

MESA: I am thinking of the boat which brought us, and its own smoke that it disappeared into when we watched it leave.

YSÉ: It is not a boat you are holding in your arms, but a living woman.

MESA: O Ysé, don't let me come back!

YSÉ: I am yielding to you. I am yours.

MESA: She said: I yield. I am yours.

YSÉ: And you have to yield to me.

MESA: I am holding it, ready to leave on it. I am holding my huge boat.

YSÉ: Is that enough? Or is there still something else you want to ask me for?

MESA: And behold I have taken her! And I hold her very body in my arms and it does not draw away from me and inside me I can hear her heart beating. There it is! It is true that she is only a woman, but I am only a man, and the

[87]

time has come when I can struggle no more, and I am like someone famished who can not hold back his tears at the sight of food to eat. Column that her body is! Power of my beloved! My meeting her is bitter and sacred and unjust and detestable. What name can I give her? Mother, because she is good to have? And sister? I hold her in my hands, a smooth female column. A prey? The odor of her life mounts to my head through my nose and I tremble at feeling her the weakest of all prey, like an animal that bends, held by the nape of its neck! Such a strange feeling! What has been done to me, what has been put into my arms which is like someone bent over? In the foreboding of my arms, it is like someone sleeping who knows all. Tell me, O presence and power of someone sleeping who knows all, if you are the woman I love. You were once in the way and I shouldn't have met you. Now you love me and you are mine, and my heart beats desperately because it knows what I am holding.

YSÉ: You are holding me and I am holding you. Although my flesh trembles, I do not draw away and I remain subdued. This is the woman

[88]

Edwige Feuillère and Paul Claudel. First performance of PARTAGE DE MIDI, *Théâtre Marigny 1948.*

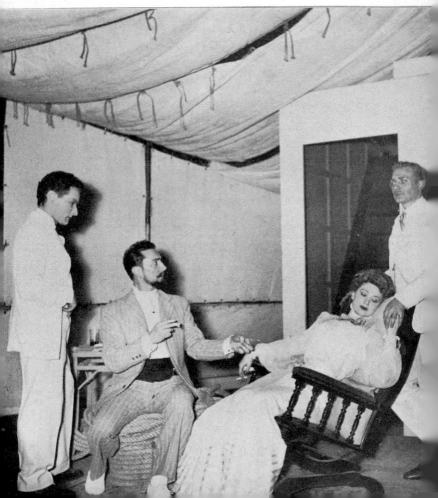

Presse Bernand

Jean Louis Barrault (Mesa), Pierre Brasseur (Almaric), Edwige Feuillère (Ysé), and Jacques Dacqmine (De Ciz). Act I, PARTAGE DE MIDI.

Pierre Brasseur and Edwige Feuillère, Act I, PARTAGE DE MIDI.

Jean Louis Barrault and Edwige Feuillère,
Act I, PARTAGE DE MIDI.

Jean Louis Barrault and Edwige Feuillère,
Act II, PARTAGE DE MIDI.

Jacques Dacqmine (as Almaric) with Edwige Feuillère in a revival of PARTAGE DE MIDI *at Théâtre Sarah Bernhardt, 1957. Act III.*

Jean Louis Barrault and Edwige Feuillère,
Act III, PARTAGE DE MIDI.

Presse Bernand

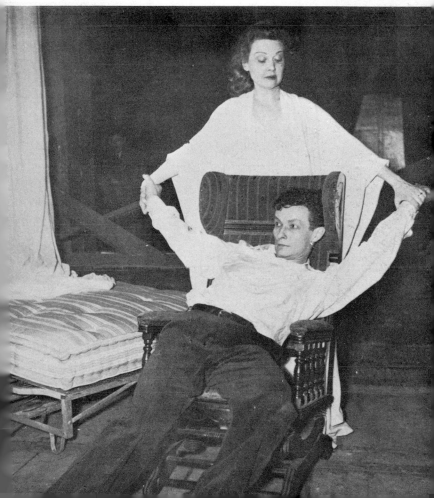

Jean Louis Barrault, Paul Claudel, Edwige Feuillère, and Pierre Brasseur. First performance of PARTAGE DE MIDI *1948.*

Presse Bernand

you found so proud and so wicked. You do not
know what a woman is and how miraculously
with all the manners she has, it is easy for her
to yield and suddenly find herself abject and
submissive and waiting, and heavy and numbed
and speechless in the hand of her enemy and
unable to move a finger. O Mesa, you are no
longer merely a man, you belong to me who
am a woman. You and I are now the same and
we feel the same heart beating in the body of
each of us. We are someone using a single heart
in order to be two. We have no names now.
There is no longer any Mesa. And Ysé? Now
there is no longer any Ysé. It is not right for me
to understand Mesa, and I must not be called
by words people know, but by other words, so
strange, like those in dreams which are noise-
less, words I cannot understand, nor by my
name either, my poor false name. Only as you
say it, Ysé, so that the words will not reach
me anywhere else save in my heart, and there
they rest heavy, as heavy as the unknown child
a woman carries when she is pregnant.

MESA: I will not scold you any more, Ysé.

YSÉ: Is that true? Are you satisfied now, professor? You won't reprimand me any more?

MESA: What a poor professor I was!

[89]

YSÉ: Did I profit or not from your lessons, professor? Tell me, Mesa, isn't it better not to feel superior to anyone, but to feel as weak as possible, someone in the arms of a woman that he will use and he will teach her to use them: me, for example, in the arms of this strong man.

MESA: I am not a strong man, Ysé. But I was a man of desire, desperately yearning, in the depths of my being, for happiness. Is it possible that you are happiness? No. You are what is in the place of happiness. When I recognized you, I began to tremble and my soul gave over. I love you, and I say that I love you, and I hear myself say that I love you, and I can resist no longer. I marry you not piously but in wickedness, O beloved who are not happiness! No more than the tree or the sacred beast for its female, have I a word by which to call you my wife. But you are here like someone I knew in my sleep, at the moment of betrayal. Like the goldworker under the lamp, you come with the breath of midnight bringing a white moth.

YSÉ: Mesa now is the man who loves someone else.

MESA: A man who is caught.

YSÉ: A man who is mine. A man I hold in my

hand. A man slung over my shoulder like a heavy slain animal. [*She lightly kisses him on the forehead.*] You know, Mesa, it is ridiculous to be a woman. Can you ever excuse this creature for being a woman?

MESA: The woman I was expecting.

YSÉ: You must understand that a woman is a creature with arms and legs. But you will see that everything about her is better and more beautiful and kinder than you think. Now, the principal thing is to become used to her.

MESA: During all those years when I was waiting for you, I did nothing but think of you and become used to you. All the hours and the minutes in bed when I held you in my arms. A dog in the moonlight used to yelp. All night long.

YSÉ: A woman is like a vase you long to buy at the shopkeeper's. A pretty vase. Impossible to live without it. And the next day, you'd be so relieved if the shopkeeper would be willing to take it back. You'd pay him to take it back. Is it a Kang shi or a Kienlung vase? Do you see? An amateur like you who keeps his eyes skinned has to look closely to be sure before buying.

MESA: Fresh and cool like a rose! Clear as the

[91]

rising sun! Like the sun which this morning had the fine idea of rising naked!

[*Gongs in the distance.*]

YSÉ: At this moment it doesn't seem to be plain sailing for the sun, at least for this sun! And tomorrow there won't be any sun at all! Nothing but a cumbersome woman, not easy to put up with. Not a vase you put in the living room, but something else.

MESA: Tomorrow? There is no tomorrow! It's today I am living and you too.

YSÉ: Look at the man who is speaking! Look at the greedy eyes of the man who says that to me! I know those greedy eyes and for a long time I have been waiting for them to look at me and to do me harm! Yes, to do me no good!

[*She lightly kisses each eyelid.*]

MESA: There is no tomorrow.

[*Ysé and Mesa clasp hands. One steps back and the other advances. The finesse of the acting is in the sentiment of the moment when one is drawn or pushed ahead. There is a halt and a kind of twisting on the spot.*]

YSÉ: You are right! There is no tomorrow. That is what you should have told me immediately.

[92]

It is not your face I like but your greedy eyes which look at me with hate. Tell me, Mesa, Monsieur the Custom-house officer, haven't we just about had enough of the whole miserable business here? Just wait for one second while I put my mouth on yours and you will know everything. There is no past now, and no future, no husband, no children, nothing, nothing, *nada!* nothing at all! You want to know the reason? I am the reason. Now tell me if that isn't what you expected.

MESA: You are the reason.

YSÉ: I am the reason. I am Ysé, your soul. The others don't count. But you are unique and I am too. I hear your voice deep within me like a cry which cannot be endured, and I rise painfully toward you like something huge and heavy, blind and full of desire and silent. What we want is not to create but to destroy and ha! [*A wild cry.*] So there'll be nothing else but you and me. Nothing in you but me, and nothing in me but what you possess: rage, compassion, the will to destroy you and to be no longer troubled in our loathsome way by the clothes of our flesh, and the cruel teeth in my heart. But they are not cruel! Ah! it is not happiness I bring you, but your death

[93]

and mine with it. But what difference is it
to me that I make you die and that I bring
death to myself and to everything provided
that at that price which is you and me when
we are given and thrown down, uprooted,
lacerated, consumed, I can feel your soul, for
one moment which is eternity. Touch [*pause*]
and take my soul like quick lime compelling
the sand as it burns and hisses! [*Mesa frees
himself abruptly.*] What is it?

MESA: Nothing. I thought someone was calling
me.

      [*Pause.*]

YSÉ [*slowly, deliberately*]: There is no one
here calling you and no one who resembles
you. But before you knew me, I was here.
Someone who called you and whom you remembered.

MESA: I remember.

YSÉ: Well, tell me about it . . .

MESA: What should I tell you?

YSÉ: Everything. We need to know everything
about each other. Your whole life. Didn't we
recognize one another on the boat immediately? Your whole life. What transpired for
me when you weren't there, and what transpired for you when I wasn't there. Now I'm

[94]

here. Ysé has come. You can't get around that.
She is here. You see, Mesa, we've arranged
all this as best we could. The two of us are
together. We finally carried off this business of
meeting, in spite of everything! And don't
think that I am going to let you go and let
you slip out of these two beautiful hands, my
right hand and my left hand. People don't
separate like that after they have spent such
a long time reaching one another.

MESA: There is no one else in the world.

YSÉ: There is no one else in the world except
you and me, and Smith who is looking at us.
You might call him the mayor, Monsieur le
Maire, presiding over our marriage.

[*Bows.*]

MESA: That's a cruel joke.

YSÉ: I like pinching you from time to time, my
little Mesa. You remember on the boat when I
cursed and it horrified you. No, this isn't a
marriage, but it's a sort of idea the two of us
had together. Why not? A superb idea! Only
Smith agrees. And here is the young girl coming to the home of her husband with her vir-
ginity, and with enough furniture to fill a
moving van. The rest will come next week.
But what I bring you is my name and my

[95]

honor—after all, I had that also—and the name and the joy of that man I married, and my poor children! As for you, well, I know they are things so great they can't be said. Each of us had his own idea. Why not! I am the woman who is forbidden. We'll see what is going to happen. Look at me, Mesa, for I am the woman who is forbidden.

MESA: I know.

YSÉ: Am I less beautiful and less desirable because of that?

MESA: No, you are not.

> [*They have come in front of the cross which Mesa earlier placed on the wheelbarrow.*]

YSÉ: Swear it! [*She raises her arm with his. Here begins the important theme of the raised arm.*] I swear that you are mine, and that I will not let you go and that I am yours. Yes, in the face of all, I swear I shall not cease being the woman who had to come. Yes, even if I were to be [*she looks at him*] damned. It is not our fault that we met on the boat. Someone took aim at us together on the boat. That is not our fault. Yes, even if I were to be . . .

> [*He puts his hand over her mouth.*]

MESA: Don't say that terrible word.

YSÉ: Well, here are some other words. [*Half-voice.*] That man, who is called my husband and whom I hate, must not stay. You must send him off somewhere, wherever you wish, and not let him come back, and not let him be seen any more. If he dies, it will be a good thing.

MESA: That would not be right.

YSÉ: Right? That depends on the point of view. For the point of view has changed a bit, dear Mesa!

MESA: I believe that in his heart he himself of his own free will wants to go to that place I spoke to him about.

YSÉ: Then why should we stand in his way? [*She sees her husband coming. With the sweetest smile.*] All the better if he dies! All the better if he. . . .

　　　　[*De Ciz enters.*]

DE CIZ: Hello!

　　　　[*The two men shake hands as Ysé watches them.*]

YSÉ: Mesa, this is my husband who is here for business. I know that business doesn't interest you in the least! Félicien, this is the custom-house officer, Monsieur le Commissaire des Douanes. Look at him closely. [*She takes his hand.*] He is suspicious and is keeping an eye on you. He can't be taken in! He is very clever. But he's boring and troublesome. Since you are here, I am giving him to you. Keep him. I'm off! I want to look at my grass cloth, you remember, the blue and white we looked at together the other day? It's the address you gave me, Mesa, the fat Cantonese, Ah Fat —Oh God, no! not Ah Fat! What a mistake! I mean Ah Toung! Goodby, Monsieur De Ciz. Your servant. [*He tries to take her hand, but she holds out her cheek and he kisses it.*] Goodby, Mesa! [*She gives him her hand.*] You must come to see me when my husband is away. I'm a widow. Don't forget. I am a widow.

[*Leaves.*]

MESA: How is your business, De Ciz?

DE CIZ: Only fairly good. It's a strange country. Everything happens differently than you expect.

MESA: Is it true that you know this fellow Ah Fat?

DE CIZ: I know him and then I don't know him. . . .

MESA: Yet in a way you do know him. Well, I advise you to know him as little as possible.

You will soon learn that there is nothing to get from the Chinese. I've heard that you're leaving. Where are you going?

DE CIZ: I'm going to Manila.

MESA: Well, let me take you to the boat.

DE CIZ: No, no, I couldn't let you. It leaves very early.

MESA: Have you thought about what I was telling you the other day?

DE CIZ: Yes, I have.

MESA: And what did you decide? I have to know.

DE CIZ: It's my wife who insists. I can't abandon her. Of course, that other matter you propose isn't brilliant, but it's stable. Yes, I think I will accept the proposition you very kindly made me.

MESA: Are you serious?

DE CIZ: I am.

MESA: I'll make arrangements then. I think you have made a good decision.

DE CIZ: I hope so. It isn't exactly what I had dreamed of.

MESA: I know. You are a poet, an imaginative man. But you have the responsibility of a family. You have to be practical.

DE CIZ: That is what I hear day in and day out.

MESA: So now, I will have to find someone for the railroad. There is a tremendous job for someone. What it demands is courage. Common sense and initiative. Someone like Amalric. What is he doing now?

DE CIZ: I think he's back on his plantation.

MESA: There's a man for you!

DE CIZ: He's a brute and a talker.

MESA: You have other qualities. You are flexible and sensitive. You would have your way with the natives. They feel at ease with you. That's why I thought of you.

DE CIZ: What exactly is this job you are offering me at the Customs?

MESA: A desk. Desk-work. You won't have to direct men or carry out any great enterprise. You will simply have to be punctual. If only we did the work ourselves, directly on the fluting of the merchandise, using a long needle or forcibly with raps of the mallet breaking a board or taking a sample with the siphon! It's a trade for a man who knows the ways of men, who holds the pursestrings. But the clerk, fitted up with his table, sadly checks the revenue. Well, the job isn't to your taste or to mine, but you have to earn your living and your family's. Security, dear Félicien, what else is there! Safety first!

DE CIZ: I am not a machine. I understand the situation now. If this mission succeeds, I will have security.

MESA: Stop thinking about it.

DE CIZ: Give me more time to think it over.

MESA [*putting his hand on his shoulder, affectionately*]: No, Félicien! I am speaking to you like a friend, believe me! [*He looks at him steadily*.] The country is bad. Pirates, poverty, wood fever and danger from poisoning is not excluded, very few means to help you at the beginning. I wouldn't hesitate myself, but I am not married. Madame De Ciz urged me not to let you take it. It's true that only the first year or two are hard. After that, there's no reason why she shouldn't come with you.

DE CIZ: My wife has nothing to do with this and I know what I have to do. [*Pause*.] Mesa, I am your man. I'll take it.

MESA: You need more time to think it over.

DE CIZ: I've thought it over. Once my mind is made up, you can count on me.

MESA: It's you alone who want this. Remember that you are leaving against my wish and advice.

[101]

DE CIZ: I understand, Mesa. I forgive you.

MESA [*with a heavy sigh*]: Have your own way!

        [*He rubs his hands.*]

DE CIZ: You are a real friend.

MESA: A sincere friend.

DE CIZ: A good sincere friend.

MESA: You won't find another one like me.

        [*De Ciz holds out his hand but Mesa embraces him clapping his hand on the back in the Brazilian style.*]

ACT III

A Confucian temple in a small Chinese port. It has been seriously destroyed. A large opening on the left through which the sky can be seen. Bags of earth piled up. It is where the Yang Koui-tzei have taken refuge, with their furniture. A kitchen table, a bed with mosquito netting, a large mirror, a wardrobe with mirror, and the famous rocking-chair of the first act. In a corner on a stool is a picture of the Virgin of Czestochowa. In front of it are two candles stuck into bottles. Ysé is reclining in the rocking-chair with knitting on her knees. Steps are heard. Amalric comes in from back stage. She half turns toward him and holds out her arms. All this is done slowly. A long embrace. When he tries to get up, she holds him back violently. He shouts:

AMALRIC: Ouch!
YSÉ: Did I hurt you, mon chéri?
AMALRIC: It's nothing. Those old guns have an absurd recoil. My shoulder is out of joint. And

I'm filthy with dirt. I am going to take a bath.

YSÉ: I love you.

AMALRIC: Look! The sun is going down, Ysé.

YSÉ: What about it? Let it go down.

AMALRIC: It's leaving us. It has business some-where else. It's over now. It will never be brought back to us. That is the pity of it.

YSÉ: It was a good sun. I have to admit that. It did us good service. It's the only one we had. It's hard to say goodby to it. It's like a big yellow beast, [*She is standing near Amalric. She is really the sun.*] laying its head on your shoulder. And you softly rub it with your cheek. Goodby, my fine sun! We loved one another, you and I! Is it true, Amalric, that we are going to die?

AMALRIC: Yes, I have to acknowledge that we are.

YSÉ: Die! A strange thought! The word sounds strange. There isn't the slightest chance of escape?

AMALRIC: Not the slightest. We are in a trap. [*He winks.*] Omega! [*He makes the gesture of slowly embracing something in his arms.*] Up till now they've spared us. In a way, they like me. And I like them. They aren't bad. They're good people, you know. But now that their

[106]

friends have been killed, it's our turn and we are out of luck. Nothing can be done. It's routine.

YSÉ: But they won't take us alive, will they?

AMALRIC: Have no fear, darling!

YSÉ: Ah! I can still hear those terrible cries when they broke into the Club yesterday. How fast it went up in flames! And that woman who jumped from the roof! It was ugly to see all those yellow bodies swarming like worms on a cake. They didn't seem to have real blood. What is it you say for rubber? *Latex*, is it? It was like milk from those terrible plants growing in the rubbish heap.

AMALRIC: You talk like a woman. It is strange, you know, but I like them. I like them very much. All you have to do is crowd them together and push. They fill your boat in bulk, like wheat. They flow into the boat. There's no empty space between them. My recruiting was progressing right on schedule. Now it's over! I'm through with coconuts, and through with rubber. What a spectacular idea it was for me to come here.

[*He sighs.*]

YSÉ: You won't let me be taken alive? Listen to me! [*She seizes him by the waist. Confused noise outside.*] Listen! Ta! ta! That's what they're shouting! Ta! ta! Do you hear it?

AMALRIC: It's nothing! There's no reason to dig your nails into my flesh. They're liquidating yesterday's business. Probably the missionaries. The remaining missionaries.

YSÉ: Are they going to come here?

> [*There is a hole in the floor, and Amalric is holding a large package wrapped in a newspaper.*]

AMALRIC: I tell you there's nothing to fear. The other day we gave them a warm reception. There is some devilry going on. The boy I used to have came to me yesterday to explain it all. It is some witchcraft about a fox or a pig. And tomorrow will be too late. There will be no one left. It will be over! The Yang Koui-tzei will have gone, flown away!

YSÉ: Did you get the right amount?

AMALRIC: The gelatine is superb. You saw it work the other day, when my mine exploded. I am proud to say it was a beautiful job. It will uproot the storeroom like a little volcano. A beautiful idea, isn't it? It's better than dying on a porcelain shovel! We won't die. We'll disappear in a clap of thunder. Pêle-mêle, bodies and souls, with the business stock and the furniture and the great quaking, we'll break through the roof in a roar. The dog, the cats, you and me, and the brat with us! [*She looks at him angrily.*] Oh! what a look! I like telling you these little things, because then something passes over your face like the flame from a canon-shot that can't be heard because it is too far off. Don't get mad. May I ask you why you insist on going on with that eternal knitting?

YSÉ: You mean that soon the infant won't need it. That is true. He is very sick.

AMALRIC: At any rate . . .

YSÉ: Leave me alone. Let me knit. That's all I can do. It's my way of praying.

AMALRIC: But I also love your child. Isn't it mine now?

YSÉ: Yes.

AMALRIC: As if I had made it. It has no other father but me. I took you and I took him with you. You are mine and he is mine, and that's the end of the story. Period. That's the end. A diplomatic period. When I found you again on the boat, I said, "This is too much of a joke! Here she is again under my nose. I must stop this." You were even more beautiful. That was bad luck. You didn't have to be a weak woman. Yes, yes, in spite of your eyes of a tigress, you know that I am stronger. As it is written! I didn't ask your opinion. Proud Ysé! with her hats and her chaise longue and bursts of laughter and her airs of a queen. I took her just the same, and she followed behind, quiet and affectionate and faithful, with that big devil of a man who walked ahead, his nose in the air! And what about the husband? There was no more husband. And the children? What children? I suppose someone is taking care of them. And the last lover, [*He is in the hole putting everything in order for the mine.*] like a piece of fruit you are finished eating, when you wipe your mouth, there remains a slight after-taste. Like your fingers in the finger-bowl when there is a bit of lemon. Some people prefer a geranium leaf.

YSÉ: You know it isn't true. You say that in order to hurt me! You know I am not as bad as that. You know I love my children. You know that I planned to have them with me. You told me I could take them back.

AMALRIC: God! The things I said which I didn't know I said!

YSÉ: And here I am with you. I wish I knew how this happened.

AMALRIC: Poor Ysé! It's unfortunate to be a

mere woman! [*He gets up and kisses her on the forehead.*] Make me some tea. [*He moves toward the opening and while Ysé prepares the tea, he looks out with his hand over his eyes.*] Nothing but the rice-field turning green and the river turning to flames. The tide of night is rising . . . [*He turns and sees her sobbing near the kettle, her head in her arms.*] Pigeon, what's the matter?

YSÉ: O Amalric, you are hard! O God! O Heaven! it is hard!

AMALRIC: Don't cry, little girl! [*She takes his hand and puts it on her brow. Gradually she quiets down.*] The water is going to boil over. [*She gets up, puts the tea in the tea-pot, pours the water. He watches her.*] What a good housewife you would have made!

YSÉ: Yes, wouldn't I, chéri? Like every other woman, I was made to live peacefully and be well protected. You can see I'm a good wife for you.

AMALRIC: Yes, I grant you that.

YSÉ: After all, it's good to think we are going to die, and that no one will come in here again, and that the house is all closed up. There is no one who will ever again call me names or hurt me. Are they true, all the things I have done?

[111]

Was it me or someone else? I deceived my husband and left him. I left my poor children with the maid, and I don't even know where they are. And that poor fellow I loved, and who loved me more than his life. As soon as I left him, I deceived him, I gave myself to you right away, as if some urgent duty were pushing me on, and I was then carrying his child.

AMALRIC: Mesa must have been baffled. It makes me laugh when I think of it.

YSÉ: He knows everything now. I still remember those last letters I received before they closed the harbor. I'm a poor wretch of a woman. What do I know? What can they ask me? What could I do? It's not my fault if all these people cling to me. A wicked woman, they'll say. Well, at least now everything is arranged so that she will harm no one in the future.

AMALRIC: There's only one cup.

YSÉ: All I had was just a pinch of tea. It's not very good, mon pauvre chéri. I don't feel hungry or thirsty. You drink. You can take all the milk left in the bottle. The child doesn't need it. I am hungry and thirsty for something else, hungry for the end of my life to come when there will be no one left to scorn me.

[112]

AMALRIC: I'd like to know what they would scorn you for.

YSÉ: You are kind, Amalric. I know that I've done nothing bad. When I try to think, and when you explain it to me, I see clearly that I did what I had to do and that things could not have been otherwise. And I think that, for Mesa, I did him a good turn when I left him. How did he know where I was? I sacrificed myself for him. But you see, Amalric, it's too hard to reason things out for oneself. There are times when it is too much for me to stand, and I have no more strength, and I am too lonely, too cut off and separated from what I love. Then I am too unhappy, and too much punished, and I pray to die, and I'm afraid of dying, and I am happy to die.

AMALRIC: Is it that hard, Ysé?

YSÉ: No, dear heart, it is not hard. With you here it is not hard. I regret nothing and I am happy. I don't really care. I have no children and no friends. I horrify everyone. I am going to die, and I am happy that there is nothing left, except the two of us alone. [*In a low voice.*] But it is terrible to be dead. Amalric, tell me the truth. Are you sure that there is no God?

[113]

AMALRIC: Why should there be? If there was one, I would have told you.

YSÉ: Good. We won't speak of it again.

AMALRIC [*Clicks his heels and salutes the icon.*]: Save for the respect we owe Madame!

YSÉ: Don't say that. Don't be a fool. [*Thoughtful and convinced.*] It is good to have nothing to reprove myself for. What I did, I would do over. That man I married is to blame. And yet there are moments when it's as if you saw there was someone constantly looking at you, and you can't escape, and whatever you do, for example, if someone laughs, or if you kiss me, he is a witness. He looks at us at that very moment. God, is that worthy of You? Does a woman need something so solemn and serious? Patience, patience, one more brief moment, and we won't be here. Yes, Amalric, when we walk, our foot makes a sound. It's as if you are walking in the night and you can't see clearly. But you hear there is a wall on the right somewhere.

AMALRIC: You're talking the way Mesa does. They are absurd dreams. Let your good Lord look at us as much as He wants to, that's His business. But I say He doesn't look at us. I saved you from Mesa. You weren't made for him. You and I are creatures of reality. No dream, just realities. Do you understand when I say reality. That is the only thing that is true! There's the sun which during all this time has finished with the business of setting. Can a man live without the sun? It's as if we were all a part of it.

YSÉ: He wrote me terrible letters. I wonder where he found all those things he said. But he is unjust with me. His child which I bore is mine. But what difference does that make to a man? I knew that I was hurting him and I left him. I did the right thing. It was for his good. Yes! I sacrificed myself for him. [*Sighs.*] With him I didn't know where I was headed. And I wanted to live. Then I met you on the boat, and I clung to you, and I thought that you were life itself, that you would save me and that I could live with you, sanely and honestly like everyone else, sincerely, peacefully, reasonably.

AMALRIC: You might say that that is just how things turned out.

YSÉ: Yes, almost. Everything is right. Suddenly, all the life a woman can give, I am giving it up in death with you, but why did he make me leave as soon as he knew I was in love? Should he have left me for one moment? With all of his being, but secretly and slyly he wanted me to leave. Did he think I couldn't read that in his eyes? It is true that I had to leave. I asked him if he was happy, and he looked at me with that expression on his face of a bad priest.

AMALRIC: Did he really love you?

YSÉ: He loved me as you will never love me. And I loved as I will never love you. Duty joins me to you because I am loyal and I know what I did. But with him it was despair and desire, a sudden gust of wind, a kind of hate, when the flesh contracts and pushes from the depths my womb like the child that is being wrenched out. You enslaved me, but you don't know what a woman is who is not enslaved. You don't know the desert of a woman, and the thirst, and the pain of love, and the knowledge that the other is alive, and the moment when each looks into the eyes of the other. You don't know what it is when another soul is thrust into yours. One whole year! [*Pause.*] It lasted one whole year. I felt he was a captive but I did not own him and there was something foreign and impossible in him. . . . He has nothing to reproach me with, because he did not give himself and I withdrew. Yet my life went on. I too had the right to live and see the earth's sun again, and live again that life which belongs to everyone, and escape from that love which is death. That is what happened. And I accept everything.

AMALRIC: Ysé, I love you. [*He kisses her lowered head.*] It is time for me to make the rounds again. The night is still ours.

[*He leaves. Pause. Darkness crossed by moonlight. The candle burns before the icon. Ysé keeps the knitting on her lap. Noiselessly Mesa appears in the doorway. Ysé does not move and does not look at him. His lips move and finally his voice is audible.*]

MESA: Didn't you receive my letters during this past year? All my letters? Why did you never answer me? Not a single word from you! Nothing! Not one single line! What had I done that you made me suffer as I did? What did I do to you? But now I have found you here. That is all I ask. You are here. I am asking for nothing and I make no reproaches. You are here, and I can see you and that is all I want. Ysé, I love you. [*During the entire scene, Ysé remains impassive, without looking at him. She knits.*] I wanted you to leave. You had guessed there was something false in me. I know what it is to do without you. You are my heart and my soul and the failings of my soul. You are the flesh of my flesh, and I cannot live without you. I don't believe what I was told. How cruel not to send me one word! I know now, I am certain you are going to explain everything. [*He swallows.*] Excuse me for those last frightful letters. I was out of my mind. I don't believe that you have stopped loving me. No, Ysé, I do not believe it. No, my love, no! Just speak, and turn toward me. Say one word that I can hear and die from joy. You see, I lost you, and now I have found you again! [*Pause.*] What have I done to you? Why do you treat me this way? Giving me no answer, as if I no longer existed! If I were in the dwelling place of the dead, I would recognize you. Ysé, can't you hear the sound of my voice? That is your name, Ysé. What have I done to you? Is your heart of stone, or of wood? Tell me what I have done wrong. Do I deserve this? I have given you everything. Tell me what I have held back. Tell me so that I will know. I gave you my body and my soul, my soul to do with as you wish. My soul as if it were mine, you took, as if you knew what it was and what it is used for. And if I made you go away, you

know it had to be. You said so yourself, for
Ciz was away and we would have fixed everything up. Then there would have been only a
few months and I would have joined you.
There were months when I did not know
where you were. Not a word! Not a word
from you! But now I am telling you Ciz is dead
and I can take you for my wife. We can love
now without hiding and without remorse.
[*Pause.*] Don't my words reach you? Is it true,
Ysé? Is your love over? I received a terrible
letter! No, Ysé, I refuse to believe it. Beloved,
it isn't true, is it? It's all over and all is forgotten. We won't think of the past. You are
here in this room and you are my beloved.
Come. I know how to take you back. You will
never leave my heart. Stand up and let me save
you from death. Can't you see that I've come
into your presence. [*Pause.*] You must believe
me. I am an old Chinese and I know all secrets.
On me there is a sign, not money, which everyone respects. Take your child, who is our
child, after all! Don't you hear me? Is life so
small a thing? Come. I am bringing you life.
[*Pause.*] Come. I will save you. If you don't
want me, let me at least bring you back to your
children. [*Pause.*] So, it is true, after all. You

[119]

are in love with that man. You no longer love me but hate me. You love him and you are his mistress. You prefer death with him to life with me. Yet you were in love with me. When you were leaving that day, I tried to kiss you on the cheek, and it was you, all tears, who deliberately took my mouth with yours. Two weeks, only two weeks. [*Pause. Low.*] Slut! Tell me what went through your mind when you gave yourself for the first time to that stray dog, when you were pregnant with another man's child, and when the first signs of life in my child mingled with your frenzy and the excitement of two adulteries? My soul which I had given you and my life seed I had planted in you were prostituted to another man. What were your thoughts when you grew heavy with my child, and when you would bring him to that man and sleep in his arms, while the limbs of my son filled you? Isn't there some stirring of pity in you now? Don't make me commit a crime. You don't realize how close you and I are to damnation at this moment. Just give me one small sign. [*Long pause. He places the candle close to her and examines her.*] You're the same woman, Ysé, but there is no great noon day sun above us. Do you re-

[120]

member our ocean? and later on, that boat we used to watch together setting out in the smoke? Now the lamp of the tomb colors your cheeks and ears and the corner of your forehead, and your hair. It's the same hair. How I remember its smell when I sank into you as into a cavern of the earth! The same hair, and deep silver strands mingle with the gold. [*He blows out the lamp.*] I've put out the lamp, and at the same time the last sun of our love went out, the last sun of noon and August, under which we said goodby, in the devouring light, and separated while desperately making signs over the distance growing wider between us. Goodby, Ysé! You did not know me. You were not able to uproot the great treasure contained in me, or take it, and I could not give it. It is not my fault. But perhaps it is. It is our fault and our punishment. I should have given everything, and I wasn't able to. That is what you did not forgive. [*Pause. He speaks to the reflection in the mirror.*] I did not love you as a pastime. Oh! Ysé! how solemnly I bore you in my heart and what comfort you found in my heart! If I had been here, I should have defended you and no one would have taken you out of my life. Do I have to stand this? She will

[121]

not speak. She is close by, and yet she isn't. She is here but she is not here. One night I saw you walking gaily and proudly toward me and you said with a mysterious smile, "It is a great mystery, Mesa. Our child has been born." I cried and laughed and could only think: it is you! Cruel Ysé, why didn't you write to me? Like someone who knows and says with her lips, "be silent!" You answered only with a smile, and I watched you smile. And now all is horror. [*Pause*.] You don't have the right. You are not alone. It is not true that you forgot me. It is not true your love is over. It is not true you hate me. There is no way out, Ysé. Can I take back what I gave you? Am I not with you wherever you are? Do you have the right not to be mine? What is in you that you haven't given me, and which I did not take and eat and breathe, and which did not nourish me on vitriol and tears and despair? Answer me. See how I suffer. Turn your face toward me, my beauty, and tell me it is not true. [*Pause*.] Ysé, what did you do with our child? [*Pause*.] Is he dead? He can't be. The knitting you have in your hands is for a child. [*Pause*.] You won't let him die, will you, Ysé? Give me my child and let me save him. [*Pause.*] Is he dead? Did you kill him? [*Pause.*] If he is here, I can find him.

> [*He moves toward the door. Footsteps of Amalric outside. He comes in.*]

AMALRIC: Who is there?

MESA: Mesa!

> [*Amalric comes forward. He strikes a match and the two men look at one another as it burns.*]

AMALRIC: You, Mesa! I am not particularly happy to see you. But I'll say hello.

> [*He lights one of the candles.*]

MESA: I have come to get this woman who is mine and the child who is mine.

AMALRIC: My friend, you will get neither one of them. I am sorry.

MESA: I will get them and you won't stop me.

AMALRIC: What a speech! How noble you are! Even in spite of her objections? What does she say? [*Mesa trembles. To Ysé.*] What do you want? To go off with him, and live, you and the child? If this is the case, stretch out your hands. [*Pause.*] Or to stay here.

MESA [*Shouting.*]: This is going too far.

> [*He makes the gesture of pulling a re-*

*volver from his pocket. Amalric takes
it away. Violent fight in the dark. Mesa
falls. Ysé has not moved.*]

YSÉ [*with a strange voice and without moving*]:
Murderer!

　　　　[*Amalric gets the candle and leans over
　　　　Mesa's body which he examines.*]

AMALRIC: Just what I thought! I dislocated his
right shoulder. But I'm sure he has injured some
other part of himself. The awkward fool! It's
curious. [*He puts back the candle in its place.*]
I say it's curious how you understand someone
when you fight with him. In one minute Mesa
and I understood one another better than in a
lifetime spent side by side. I apologize for the
incident.

YSÉ [*standing and looking at the inert body*]:
Amalric, it's ghastly and ugly! Don't leave him
on the floor that way like a disjointed puppet.
You can't do that.

AMALRIC: How did he get here?

YSÉ: I heard he had a pass on him.

AMALRIC: That's interesting. [*Amalric goes
through his pockets and removes a kind of
small board strangely cut out which he shows
to Ysé.*] I shouldn't be surprised if we've been
rescued.

[124]

YSÉ: Rescued?

AMALRIC: You say that sadly.
   [*He looks at her.*]

YSÉ: I learned also that my husband is dead. We can be married, Amalric.

AMALRIC: Good! It's been a fine evening. We'll make an excellent couple in the eyes of the law.

YSÉ: Is there no way for us to take him with us?

AMALRIC [*harshly*]: That's impossible.

YSÉ: We can't leave him to the Chinese.

AMALRIC: Bah! He'll blow up instead of us. The time bomb is set. We have only to let it tick on.

YSÉ: It's wrong, Amalric, we can't leave him like this on the floor all crumpled up.

AMALRIC: You're right, Ysé, we can't leave him like this on the floor all crumpled up. I'm going to get that fine armchair, the one on which two can sit. [*He goes out and returns with a large Chinese armchair with a round back in the form of Omega.*] Here it is. We'll put him on it. He'll be comfortable. He will look like a judge. Pick him up.

YSÉ: What do you mean, pick him up?

AMALRIC: You're strong. Pick him up and set him on the chair. Don't you understand?

YSÉ: Pick him up yourself.

AMALRIC: No, I'll be the audience. There has to

be someone to look. Oh, but you're clumsy! [*Mesa is solemnly installed on the throne-chair, in the middle of the room.*] There! He really looks fine. He's quite impressive. He's all arrayed to face the events. Greetings, Monsieur le Commissaire! All we have to do now is to get the hell out.

YSÉ: You didn't see something. His billfold is on the floor.

AMALRIC: You're right, by God. His billfold is on the floor. Nothing is more definitely on the floor than that billfold.

YSÉ: There is certainly money in it.

AMALRIC: Yes, there must be. Why shouldn't there be?

YSÉ [*hatefully*]: You might as well pick it up.

AMALRIC: Yes, my angel, I might as well pick it up. Don't watch if it disgusts you. [*He makes a move to pick it up and then stands up. Ysé takes the candle and goes off, while Amalric then picks up the billfold.*] It will all go smoothly. [*Ysé returns with the candle which she places before the icon, then starts to follow Amalric. A short pause before the icon which may be interpreted in various ways. She hesitates a moment in front of Mesa. Amalric goes up to*

[126]

her, takes her by the wrist and leads her off.]
Aren't you taking the child?

YSÉ: He is dead. [*They go out. Mesa is alone,
solemnly propped up on the funeral throne.
The setting, from now on useless, gradually
gives way to the starry sky. The noise of the
stars, for they do make a noise, as all those who
have troubled to listen know, is expressed by a
low dull rumbling like that of a distant liturgy.
Like the Scripture texts which reach our ears
in a torrent of consonants, sometimes weak
and sometimes strong.*] Quis est iste involvens
sententias verbis imperitis? Ubi eras quando
appendebam fundamenta terrae . . . Etc.

> [*The Song of Mesa is composed from
> this dialogue.*]

MESA [*He has slowly recovered consciousness,
which is expressed by a rinforzando of the
stellar kettle.*]: Why? [*Muffled explanation of
the kettle.*] Why she? Why that woman suddenly on the boat, with such skill, and at that
moment? What did she have to do with me?
Did I need her? [*The kettle pretends not to
hear and is occupied with something else.*] It
was you alone! [*A silence, not the result of a
weakening, but on the contrary, of a reinforc-
ing of something positive. An acceleration of*

[127]

interest.] You didn't ask for my opinion! On your own authority! Suddenly, with all doors closed, you took command alone. What could I do? I tried. It is not easy to get the better of me. It was a clever move to have brought me that woman all of a sudden. You must have chosen her carefully. Like a fighting cock that is brought in a basket. Forty days on that boat. And for forty days there I was facing her. I had all the time in the world to look at her and learn that she was the woman I needed. Did I believe in her? for a single moment? I repeat, for a single moment? Did I believe that happiness, as the saying goes, was within my grasp? I was the prisoner who grinds his teeth and can't move. You pulled that trick all alone. Suddenly, cleverly you had the upper hand. As if —as if that thing—I mean that pact we had made together before the creation of the world —well, what happened to it? [*The kettle is about to answer, but Mesa interrupts.*] No! you on the fourth floor, don't listen. You're here and that's enough. I say it's sufficient. Just don't talk, so there will be a way of hearing you. For the one who communicates with your silence, that is fine and there's no need for explanation. [*The kettle is not pleased and*

[128]

suddenly you distinctly hear the words: The others] What do you mean, the others?

> [*The kettle, in its immense language distributed over the entire firmament, repeats.*]

VOICE: The others—the others—the others—the others. The others, for better or for worse, exist, and not just you alone. Have you finally learned that?

MESA: I've learned it. Everything was nicely set up so that I could learn it. For me it was the woman, whom I cared nothing about, the woman, and the idea of her was planted in my mind. Not only in my mind. "In my arms," as they say. Not only in my arms, she reached to my soul, as they say, and all this was done for her, to join with my soul by means of my heart and by wresting it from me! That was how she entered me and took my hand. Is it believable? Of course! "love," what is called love, of course I had heard of it, everyone does, but the real article, what it is, ah! I say this from the bottom of our abyss and there's no other answer save this supplication. I needed someone with her face to teach me, and no one else. It was worth the trouble to create the world. Yes, if that was what You didn't know and needed to learn, yes, it was worth the trouble to create the world, and the cross wasn't anything superfluous. Those three hours when at this very moment I am looking at You on the cross. [*Silence.*] I loved her, and she did that to me! [*Silence.*] Do you hear? That was done to us, comrade, to both of us. More than the heart, that living name in me which makes me, was betrayed. It was stripped from me. You know all about it, You know, O Lord, with what thirst, and gnashing of teeth, and dryness and horror and pulling I took hold of her, and then she did that to us. I swear she didn't have the right to betray both of us, to betray that hateful sacrament! "Love," they call it. They are always speaking of "love." But you know what keeps us apart, and the despair over that thing which keeps us apart, that rage, that indignation over the thing which refuses, and which separates and which says no. It is not with kisses and biting that you succeed, it is with the cross. An instrument which You are watching me slowly build. [*The kettle has begun to think of something else.*] Now she has run off, and because she ran off, she has the crazy idea that it's all over, as if a million stars were

[130]

blotted out. There aren't any walls, but there
are a million stars mounting guard around her.
That is what I gambled on. That's what I won
at the lottery. Some men have won a kingdom
in the lottery, a slice of the planet which filled
their bellies. But what I won was that soul, an
inexplicable detestable soul which is the key to
my own. It isn't a simple matter to get rid of
that soul which she mysteriously owes me, my
own desperate soul, which explains the existence of hers! She ran off, but it isn't time that
we don't have. Here I am with the million stars
close to me which are mounting guard around
her. It isn't that easy to run away from God.
It isn't my fault. At my expense I bring Him
to her. And that name within her, at her expense, I bring to her, more terrifying than hell.
Others won America, but I won that soul, and
I won it at the expense of my own whose
charge I received, and that name, my own,
which I have to ask her for and which she
alone knows.

> [*Ysé enters and stands motionless and
> erect behind Mesa's chair. He knows
> she is there. A long silence. There is no
> hurry.*]

[131]

YSÉ: Quite simply it is what is called a catch.

MESA: Ysé, you know what is going to happen. Why did you come back?

YSÉ [*She kneels behind him. Nothing penitential is implied. It is simply a more comfortable position for conversation.*]: What is called a "catch." You realize the Chinese had no time to wait, and the boat hook slipped over the slimy flagstones. The swift ebb-tide swept the boat away. I heard only one cry in the night. A kind of ridiculous cry.

MESA: I didn't need you.

YSÉ [*laughing briefly*]: It would have been too convenient. All the same, you weren't able to get rid of me. It is not that easy to get rid of me.

MESA: What about me? Was there something to settle with me?

YSÉ: Mesa, I have to tell you our child is dead.

MESA: I knew that.

YSÉ: No, you didn't know. You couldn't have known it before I told you. That is why I came back.

MESA: I know now.

YSÉ: And I came back also for something else.
      [*She takes hold of his wounded arm.*]

MESA: You're hurting me.

YSÉ: You're a softy. Just a bit of pain? You

shouldn't care. It doesn't pain more than it should.

MESA: Well, speak! I'm listening. Ysé doesn't exist. All that is left is a voice speaking behind me in the night.

YSÉ: I couldn't let you go off that way. Don't you think I heard all those terrible things you said to me just now?

MESA: Well?

YSÉ: I couldn't let you go off that way. I just couldn't. But now you can die. Listen to me, I pardon you for all those terrible things you said. I pardon you for everything. Are you glad?

MESA: And is there not something perhaps that you have to be pardoned for?

YSÉ: You mustn't ask me for more than I can give, Mesa. My dead husband, my dead children, and you too perhaps if you think I have done you harm, you are like something that has been picked up and held up at arm's length in order to see. I am looking at it. You mustn't ask me for anything more.

MESA: I want only to understand you, as if suddenly you were a new woman coming to me.

YSÉ: But didn't you love the other Ysé?

MESA: You know I did.

[133]

YSÉ: How fast that boat got away! It was swept away. I know someone who must have been very surprised. I laughed myself sick. There was a kind of cry back there. I wish you had heard it. A kind of ridiculous cry.

MESA: I am listening. I am here to listen to all you have on your heart.

YSÉ: Have I the right to take your hand?

MESA: Take it.

YSÉ: Not the right hand. The left. The one that hurts. That's the one I want. I can tell everything to the left hand.

MESA: It would be better if you were closer.

YSÉ: Do you mean there is place enough beside you in this large round chair?

MESA: There is plenty of space. It is not like the rocking-chair. You can sit beside me if you want to.

YSÉ: Will the gentleman allow me to sit down beside him on this chair?

MESA: Come. [*She sits beside him.*]

YSÉ: Tell me, Mesa, do you remember the Chinese tomb at Hong-Kong which had the shape of a hook, an Omega?

MESA: I remember it.

YSÉ: Well, this chair also is in the form of an Omega.

[134]

MESA: Just enough space for the two of us.

YSÉ: The two pincers have closed over us and we are caught! There's no way now to leave. [*Ysé is seated close beside Mesa. His left arm is around her and the back of the chair. She holds him with his right arm. For the lighting, there is a diagonal moonbeam which soon reaches the chair and then moves beyond it.*] It is better there are two of us for what is going to happen. Both of us close together as we used to be. That is what I came here for. There is no need for an explanation. My heart is beside yours, close enough for you to feel it. Can you hear? [*Low voice.*] It's beating. I came to bring you my heart. And my body, Mesa, which is warm from yours, against your body.

MESA: I have never forgotten it.

YSÉ: It is all so strange. We were made to be together. At least that was certain.

MESA: Yes.

YSÉ: But there is something else, mon petit Mesa. Something I couldn't let you leave without knowing. I had to tell you. Are you listening? Do you feel how close and comfortable I am with you at this moment?

MESA: I am listening.

YSÉ: Did you know . . .

[135]

[*During this conversation, Mesa does not look at her once.*]

MESA: Go on.

YSÉ: Did you know how much I hated you, mon petit Mesa?

MESA: Yes, I knew.

YSÉ: After all, I was glad when you made me your mistress. Félicien gave us no trouble. Now, he's dead. My children . . . I didn't want to die any more than any one else. I was young and pretty. Then it happened. You came. There was no way out. I knew there was no way out. The Omega was around us. I tried. It wasn't my fault. You can't say I didn't try. There was no way out.

MESA: That is true.

YSÉ: I tried. You can't blame me for anything. Tell me if you have ever blamed me for anything.

MESA: No, I haven't.

YSÉ: From time to time, how you hated me! I could read it in your eyes. It was a sudden hate, a terrible desperate desire for me to leave, at any cost, in any way, for me to pull myself away from you. It was your despair which made me want to live. I tried. You would never have been able to. How can you blame me?

[136]

You had the eyes of a priest which looked right through me. Did you know how much I hated you at those moments?

> [*Sweetly, tenderly, curled up against him.*]

MESA: I knew.

YSÉ: Can you feel these two hearts of ours? My heart against yours, yours against mine, my body against yours. We are going to die together, the two of us, these two hearts of ours which have a strange way of hating each other. The things we have to forgive one another for! There is too much hate for the story to close this way when we are together.

MESA: Don't trust me.

YSÉ: You're not stronger than me. You can't get rid of me this way. I'm clinging to you like an animal.

MESA: All right, I agree. All is over and I take charge. Let me pay. I've paid already.

YSÉ: Dearly!

MESA: Yes, dearly!

YSÉ: And that's what you don't like, Mesa, to pay dearly for something. We pretend to give everything while all the time deep down within us we are determined to keep everything for ourselves. That is how once you offered yourself to God, so wrapped up and tightly closed that I can't imagine how the good Lord would have gone about opening you. He would have broken the nails of His fingers. It's ugly, mon petit Mesa, to be avaricious. Ugly to be the self-centered egoist that you were.

MESA: At least you were very successful in getting what God failed to get.

YSÉ: Did I really succeed? Did I really teach you what it means to belong to someone else? Did I really teach you once and for all how you give up your miserly possessions? I was aiming at the marrow of your bones, mon petit Mesa, at your soul, as they say, at the root of your being. Someone had to do that. I ask you if you could resist the cross, Mesa, once it has begun to function like any other instrument? After all, woman was made by God, and no matter how bad she may be, she serves for some use. She too can be a cross. A great cross. You wanted only my body, but I had something quite different in mind. When you've taken everything from a woman, you have to give her something in its place. The world is very big, Mesa, but there is one thing, in spite of its bigness, that it couldn't give you.

MESA: What is that?

YSÉ: Your real name. The real name which is yours and which only I know. My soul is your name, your key, your cause. Your name is so inseparable from me that you would have to take it from me by force.

MESA: There was no way for me to give you my soul, Ysé.

YSÉ: Are you sure? [*She has gone to the other side of the chair. The moonbeam has left Mesa and reached her.*] Are you sure there was no way?

MESA: Didn't I try?

YSÉ: Yes, we tried. As best we could.

MESA: And now we're going to die.

YSÉ: You are so intelligent, Mesa. You understand everything. Yes, now we are going to die. You could die by my hand. [*She slowly stands up behind him. She raises her arm by easing successively each joint and finally her hand. Now the theme of the hand takes on its supernatural importance.*] Mesa, I am Ysé. That is why I tried to escape from you.

MESA: It is not your fault. The current was stronger than you suspected. That current is the tide of midnight.

YSÉ: Do you know that at that very moment I suddenly saw the stars in the sky. [*The moon-*

*beam has left her. They are now in the dark-
ness, and the beam has passed by.*] I had to take
that in all at once. All the stars in the sky! [*She
moves upstage, then back to Mesa.*] They hit
me square in the face, like a sun stroke.

MESA: When I was waiting for you just now,
they kept me company.

YSÉ: What are they up to, Mesa, in their useless-
ness, those stars in the sky?

MESA: What do you mean?

YSÉ: There had to be someone, I guess, to give
me all those useless stars.

MESA: I can't unhook them for you.

YSÉ: It's easy. Just stretch out your hand.

[*She stretches his hand.*]

MESA: I can't give you heaven and earth.

YSÉ: You're still a miser. Aren't heaven and earth
there to serve for some use? Are they forbidden? Take them. Give them to me. It's easy.
Just stretch out your hand. Get up!

[*She takes his hand and forces him to
get up. She raises his hand with hers, as
if it were a work difficult to accomplish
with gentleness and precaution. He has
gotten up painfully and stands erect.*]

MESA: Be quiet!

[*She sinks down at his feet in the dark.*]

[140]

YSÉ: Remember me for one moment in this darkness. I was once your vine.

> [*Pause. Silence. Only the luminous raised hand of Mesa is visible. It alone fills the hollow of the stage.*
>
> *The curtain drops like lightning.*]

NOTES

1. (p. 4) Bernard the hermit crab. This is the translation of Bernard Lhermite, the name given to a shell-fish which has the habit of crawling into the shell of another animal.
2. (p. 4) "Good-for-nothing" is the translation of *ferlampier*, a dialectical word from Claudel's native province of Champagne.
3. (p. 5) Rimbaud. For Claudel's debt to Rimbaud, see his preface to the *Oeuvre* of Rimbaud, published by Le Mercure de France.
4. (p. 7) "Her eyes . . ." This quotation seems to have been invented by Claudel.
5. (p. 10) "by God" is a translation of the phrase *Maski*, an exclamation of Polish origin.
6. "Green foliage . . ." This quotation seems to have been invented by Claudel. (p. 12)
7. (p. 13) Pondichéry is a colony in India.
8. (p. 45) "endless stretch of green" translates *verdouillade*, a popular word referring to the green fields of Normandy.
9. (p. 45) "I'm wild and woolly and full of fleas" is in English in Claudel's text. It is a quotation from an obscene English ballad.

10. (p. 47) "Toward Cimbebasia and the Oval Cities." This is a literal translation of *vers la Cimbébasie et les Villes Ovales,* which would seem to be an invention of Claudel, so devised as to resemble Rimbaud's style.

THE TIDINGS
BROUGHT
TO MARY

INTRODUCTION

In the native province of Claudel, Le Tardenois, there is a natural menhir called "Le Grès-
qui-va-boire" ("the sandstone which is going to
drink"). At sunset the shadow of this upright
stone reaches a small stream. As a child Claudel
knew how much this phenomenon was revered
throughout the countryside. By all those who
looked at it, the extended shadow was considered
the measure of the day's accomplishments. At
the various moments of his life when he wrote
or revised *L'Annonce faite à Marie*, a work that
is replete with names and memories of his province, Claudel looked upon this stream as the
source of strength, the spiritual reserve his characters draw upon. The two sisters, Mara and
Violaine, the father Anne Vercors and the
builder of churches, Pierre de Craon, all represent for Claudel that supernatural power in man
which refuses to accept death or doubt or despair. They testify to that quality of faith which

makes possible the life story of a saint and the construction of such monuments as the Gothic cathedrals.

As the work reached its definitive form, the names of villages and localities in Le Tardenois came into focus: Chinchy, Saponay, Combernon. The historical moment of the play's action became the fifteenth-century, the period of Joan of Arc and The Hundred Years War. Le Tardenois is a northern plateau in France, extending between the Marne River and the Aisne. It is a part of the larger province of Champagne where the royal highways of Soissons and Reims cross. A country of fortresses which once belonged to the Frankish kings and the Merovingian princes. It is the territory of Clovis from whom the race of the Louis' descended. In its center rises the cathedral of Reims, where the sacrament of monarchy was instituted and the kings of France were consecrated.

The term *la douce France* applies better to other regions than to Le Tardenois. Claudel often referred to the strong wind which blows there constantly, to the bleakness and the semi-wildness of the landscape. The poet was totally familiar with the life of the soil and the life of the peasants of his province. Many of the elements of his early life he put into his play: trees and harvests, the care of a large farm, horses and oxen, and ploughs, the song of the oriole and the lark, the immemorial traditions and nobility of country life.

The first version of the play was called *La Jeune Fille Violaine* and was published in 1892. The definitive version for the stage of *L'Annonce faite à Marie*, which has been followed in this translation, was published in 1948. At intervals during a span of fifty-six years, Claudel returned to the text, worked on it and revised it. In many ways, it was the work he was the most attached to, the one for which he expressed the most constant affection. The strange name of his heroine Violaine is evocative of viol and violet as well as of the mediaeval names Yolande and Ghislaine. One is inclined even to find in it a resonance from Claudel's native town Villeneuve. The idea of the play and of Violaine's miracle came to him from a book on German mystics of the 14th century and the story of a woman who miraculously fed a dead infant from her breast.

The action revolves around the relationship between the two sisters who are totally different in temperament and yet who are indissolubly joined. Violaine is the good sister who will represent Christian charity in its fullest sense. Mara (whose name in Hebrew means "bitter") is the jealous sister who will, at the end of the play, murder Violaine. Mara's infant who dies and is brought back to life by Violaine, is the child of both sisters. After the miracle the infant will have the blue eyes of her second mother. In the final revisions of the text, Claudel's interest fixed on Mara who grew in importance for him. He came to realize the absolute necessity existing between Mara and Violaine, and the need which each sister has for the other. Mara's faith in God, a violent and almost brutal faith, serves an important function in the play, that of revealing the sanctity of Violaine. The relationship between the sisters makes *L'Annonce* into a human and a supernatural drama at the same time.

This constant intermingling of the human and the supernatural makes the drama into a liturgical play. In the third act, on Christmas eve, Mara, carrying her dead child in her arms, is trying to find Violaine at the very moment of midnight mass. The resurrection of Aubaine will coincide with the birth of the Saviour. It is impossible not to evoke the importance in the life of Claudel of Christmas Eve 1886 when the drama of his conversion took place, described by him in the famous text *Ma Conversion*, and which dominated his existence. He took great liberties with the facts of history when in his play he has the consecration of Charles VII in the cathedral of Reims take place on the same Christmas eve as Violaine's miracle. (The king's consecration actually took place in the month of July.)

With Claudel's new understanding of the role of Mara, the "message" of the play, which is exaltation, became strange and clearer. In insisting that God do her some good, in forcing Him to bring her daughter back to life, Mara became the element of violence which Claudel saw in the Gospel sentence: "Ever since John the Baptist's time, the kingdom of heaven has opened to force." (*Matthew* 11:12.) This very sentence is actually the theme of the play. It is a conflict between natural forces and supernatural forces in which the latter are the more powerful. The harsh wind which blows over Le Tardenois and which caused Claudel to call his part of the world *Wuthering Heights* is in contrast with the rich land which will produce fruit and grain. In *L'Annonce faite à Marie*, the spirit of Monsanvierge and the cloistered nuns dominate the fertile farmlands of Combernon below.

L'Annonce faite à Marie was written in 1910

and first performed, under the direction of Lugné-Poe, in 1912, at the Théâtre de l'Oeuvre in Paris. In 1938, when Jacques Copeau was director of the Comédie-Française, he expressed a desire to add the play to the repertory of the theatre. Claudel began to revise the text, but he was unable to comply with the requests Copeau made for changes. The project was not completed. The letters written at this time by the poet and director are soon to be published in one of the *Cahiers Paul Claudel*, an issue to be devoted to the friendships and quarrels between Claudel and his *metteurs-en-scène*.

Charles Dullin intervened at the end of the rather painful controversy between Claudel and Copeau, and was able to convince the poet that he should completely rewrite the fourth act. This was finally done. The intermediary edition of 1940 has many changes, but the definitive edition for the stage, published in 1948, has an entirely new fourth act in which the character Pierre de Craon does not appear. This final version was prepared explicitly for the director Jacques Hébertot who presented in his own theatre, in 1948, what has been until now the most successful production of *L'Annonce*. Claudel attended the rehearsals of that production and took an active part in directing the play. During the years it had become his most popular play. The professional theatre had paid little attention to it. Claudel had seen many performances of it, in many languages, during the course of his world travels. It had been performed especially by amateur groups, church schools and church guilds. The poet has stated that often the acting and the productions made him suffer. He referred to this trial of his favorite play as *le martyre de Violaine*. Not until the first performances at the Théâtre Hébertot, in 1948, was he satisfied with a production of *L'Annonce faite à Marie*.

There were important scenic changes in the Hébertot production. For example, the prologue and acts I and II were played without interruption. And a basic stage set was used throughout the play. But the profoundest changes were in a strengthening of the structure (the new fourth act), in a clarifying of characterization, and in an emphasis on the liturgical meaning of the play.

The character of the prologue, Pierre de Craon, who was not in the original *Jeune Fille Violaine*, appears as the mysterious stranger, as the "guest," who is in reality a delegate, one sent by God in order to reveal certain truths.

[153]

His elimination from the fourth act in the definitive version, reinforces his mystical role. Pierre is the instrument of grace who will divert Violaine from her earthly destiny. He is the leper in the prologue, and Violaine's kiss to the leper is the supreme act of charity which will precipitate the action of the play. Violaine is the handmaid of the Lord (*Ecce ancilla Domini*) who submits to the will of the Creator. On one level of meaning, *L'Annonce* is a simple domestic drama, and on another level, it is a mystery play where the spirit of Monsanvierge penetrates the lives of the peasants and farmers of Combernon.

In its fullest meaning *L'Annonce* testifies to the physical-spiritual cycle of death and rebirth. The miracle of the third act, the death of Violaine and the continuing life of Mara, the vocation of Pierre de Craon who gives his life to the building of cathedrals, the king's consecration at Reims and the end of an historical period, the emptying of Monsanvierge at the end of the play and the new order which begins in Combernon, are changes which relate to an ending that is in reality a beginning. When Claudel described his deeply personal experience of Christmas eve, 1886, he said that the understanding which struck him the most forcibly at that time was the innocence of God, the eternal childhood of God. The poet's attachment to the earth, and particularly to the country of Le Tardenois, to the land of the Gothic parishes of Reims, Soissons and Laon, is visible everywhere in *L'Annonce faite à Marie*. But he knows the planet too, the smallness of the earth and its bigness, and the place of man in the darkness of the world.

WALLACE FOWLIE

PRINCIPAL EDITIONS OF

L'Annonce faite à Marie

1912   Nouvelle Revue Française.
1940   Nouvelle édition augmentée d'une variante. N.R.F.
1948   Edition définitive pour la scène. Gallimard.

PRINCIPAL PERFORMANCES

1912   Paris. Théâtre de l'Oeuvre. Directed by Lugné-Poe.
1942   Théâtre Louis Jouvet in South America. Directed by Louis Jouvet.
1948   Théâtre Hébertot. First performance of definitive version. Directed by Jacques Hébertot.

CAST

ANNE VERCORS	Jean Hervé
JACQUES HURY	Robert Hébert
PIERRE DE CRAON	Alain Cuny
APPRENTICE	Jean Pommier
THE MOTHER	Eve Francis
VIOLAINE	Hélène Sauvaneix
MARA	Carmen Duparc

PROLOGUE

DRAMATIS PERSONAE

ANNE VERCORS

JACQUES HURY

PIERRE DE CRAON

ELIZABETH VERCORS

VIOLAINE

MARA

A COMPANY OF MEN AND ANGELS

The barn at Combernon. A large building with square pillars and a framework with pointed arches. Empty except the back of the right wing which is filled with straw. Bits of straw on the earthen floor. In the back, a large double door, with a complicated arrangement of bars and locks. On the double door are painted barbaric pictures of St. Peter and St. Paul, one holding keys and the other a sword. A large yellow wax candle, stuck in an iron hook on the pillar, illuminates them.

The drama takes place at the end of the conventional Middle Ages, such as the poets of the Middle Ages might have imagined Antiquity.

End of the night and early hours of the morning.

Pierre de Craon, dressed in a black cape, enters on a large horse. His gigantic moving shadow is visible behind him on the wall, the ground and the pillars.

Suddenly Violaine comes out from behind a pillar and stands in front of him. She is tall and thin, barefoot, wearing a dress of heavy wool.

*Her head, bound in linen cloth, is in a style both
peasant and religious.*

VIOLAINE [*laughing and raising her two hands
with their index fingers crossed*]: Halt, my
lord knight! Get down from your horse!

PIERRE: Violaine!
[*He gets off his horse.*]

VIOLAINE: I'm surprised, maître Pierre! Is this
the way you take leave, like a thief, without
greeting the ladies as you should?

PIERRE: Go back into the house, Violaine. It is
still night outside and the two of us are here
alone. You know I am a man not very sure of
himself.

VIOLAINE: Stone-worker, I am not afraid of you.
It's not always easy to be wicked. It's not easy
to get the better of me! Poor Pierre! You
didn't even succeed in killing me. With that
bad knife of yours! There was only a small
cut on my arm and no one saw it.

PIERRE: Violaine, will you forgive me?

VIOLAINE: That's why I am here.

PIERRE: You were the first woman I put my
hand on. Satan was in me all of a sudden. He
knows how to profit from such chances.

VIOLAINE: But I was stronger than Satan.

[162]

PIERRE: Now I am more dangerous than I was then.

VIOLAINE: Are we going to fight again?

PIERRE: Just my simple presence here can be fatal.

[*Silence.*]

VIOLAINE: I don't understand.

PIERRE: Weren't there enough stones to put together and pieces of wood to join and metals to melt? That was my work. And yet suddenly I put my hand on the work of someone else and coveted a living soul.

VIOLAINE: In the house of my father who was your host. What would they have said if they had learned about it? But I hid you carefully. Everyone still looks upon you as a sincere blameless man.

PIERRE: God judges the heart despite appearances.

VIOLAINE: Well, it won't go beyond the three of us.

PIERRE: Violaine.

VIOLAINE: Yes, maître Pierre? [*Smiling, she stands under the candle. He looks at her for a long time.*] Have you looked at me long enough?

PIERRE: Who are you, and what is that part in

[163]

you which God has kept for Himself, for the hand that touches you with desire and the very flesh to be thus withered, as if it had drawn near to the mystery of its dwelling?

VIOLAINE: What happened to you this past year?

PIERRE: The very day after the day you remember . . .

VIOLAINE: Yes?

PIERRE: I recognized the terrible disease on my side.

VIOLAINE: What disease?

PIERRE: The leprosy that is spoken of in the book of Moses.

VIOLAINE: What is leprosy?

PIERRE: Didn't they ever tell you about that woman who long ago lived alone among the rocks of Géyn, who was covered with veils and who carried a rattle?

VIOLAINE: Is it that disease, maître Pierre?

PIERRE: It is of such a nature that the man who has caught it in all of its virulence has to be sent away at once, for there isn't a man living who if he is tainted just a bit will not grow sick with the disease.

VIOLAINE: How is it then that you still move about freely?

[164]

PIERRE: I have a dispensation from the bishop. And you know yourself that I almost never appear. Except before my workmen to give them orders. My disease is still covered up and disguised. Who, except myself, could bring to their wedding day these newly made churches which God put into my charge?

VIOLAINE: Is this why we haven't seen you at Combernon?

PIERRE: I couldn't exempt myself from coming back here, because my duty is to open the flank of Monsanvierge and split open the wall each time a new flight of doves tries to enter from the high arch whose gratings are opened only to the sky. This time we were taking to the altar an illustrious host, a solemn censer, the Queen herself, mother of the king, on behalf of her son stripped of his kingdom. Now I'm on my way back to Reims.

VIOLAINE: Maker of doors, let me open this one for you.

PIERRE: Is there no one else on the farm to do this for me?

VIOLAINE: The servant girl likes to sleep. She gave me the keys without argument.

PIERRE: Aren't you afraid and horrified of the leper?

VIOLAINE: God is here and I'm in His keeping.

PIERRE: Give me the key now.

VIOLAINE: Let me do it. You don't know how to treat these old doors. Do you think I'm one of those beautiful young ladies whose slender fingers never touched anything rougher than the spur of the new knight, as delicate as the spine of a bird, to arm his heel? Just look!

> [*She opens the two locks which grate and pulls the bolts.*]

PIERRE: That old iron is rusty.

VIOLAINE: This door is no longer used. But the road this way is shorter. [*It is hard for her to push the bar.*] I've opened the door.

PIERRE: Who could hold out against such an assailant? Look at the dust! The old door cracked and rumbled up to the very top. The spiders are scattering and the old nests are collapsing. It's opening at the middle.

> [*The door opens. Through it can be seen the countryside covered with fields and harvests in the night.*]

VIOLAINE: That little rain did some good.

PIERRE: The dust of the road will be laid.

VIOLAINE [*low voice, affectionately*]: Peace be with you, Pierre!

[166]

[*Silence. Suddenly, clear and high in the sky the first bell of the Angelus. Pierre removes his hat and both cross themselves.*]

VIOLAINE [*her hands clasped, her face toward heaven, with a beautifully clear and penetrating voice*]: Regina Caeli, laetare, alleluia!
[*second bell*]

PIERRE [*muffled voice*]: Quia quem meruisti portare, alleluia!
[*third bell*]

VIOLAINE: Resurrexit sicut dixit, alleluia!

PIERRE: Ora pro nobis Deum.
[*Pause.*]

VIOLAINE: Gaude et laetare, Virgo Maria, alleluia!

PIERRE: Quia resurrexit dominus, alleluia. [*bells*]
[*low voice*] Oremus. Deus qui per resurrectionem Fili tui Domini Nostri Jesu Christi mundum laetificare dignatus es, praesta, quaesumus, ut per ejus Genitricem Virginem Mariam perpetuae capiamus gaudia vitae. Per eumdem Dominum Nostrum Jesum Christum qui tecum vivit et regnat in unitate Spiritus Sancti Deus per omnia saecula saeculorum.

VIOLAINE: AMEN.

[*Both cross themselves.*]

[167]

PIERRE: It's early for the Angelus.

VIOLAINE: Up there in the convent they say matins when it is still night, as the Carthusians do.

PIERRE: Tonight I shall be in Reims.

VIOLAINE: Do you know the way? First keep to the hedge. Then pass that low house in the clump of elder trees where you will see five or six beehives. A hundred steps after that you reach the royal highway.

[*Pause.*]

PIERRE: Pax tibi. All of creation is with God in His deep mystery. What was hidden becomes again visible with Him. On my face I feel the cool breath of a rose. Praise the Lord, blessed land, in tears and darkness! The fruit is for man but the flower is for God and the good scent of all that is born. Like the leaf of a mint, the scent of a holy soul that was concealed has released its virtue. Farewell, Violaine, who opened this door for me, I will not return to you again. O young tree of the knowledge of good and evil, I am beginning now to draw away because I stretched out my hand to possess you. Already my soul and my body are being divided, like wine in the

[168]

vat mingled with the crushed grapes. What
does it matter? I had no need of a woman. I
have not possessed a mortal woman. The man
who in his heart preferred God sees, when he
dies, the angel who watched over him. The
time will soon come when another door will
dissolve. When this man who gave pleasure to
very few in this life goes to sleep, having
finished his work, in the arms of the eternal
Bird! When already on all sides through transparent walls appears dark Paradise. And when
the censers of night mingle with the odor of
the filthy wick as it goes out!

VIOLAINE: Pierre de Craon, I know that you
do not expect me to say "poor man" or "poor
Pierre" or to draw any false sighs. To the man
suffering, the consolations of a joyful con-
soler are not worth much, and his suffering
is not for us what it is for him. Suffer with
Our Lord. But know that your bad action is
forgiven as far as I am concerned, and I am
at peace with you. I do not scorn you and detest you because you are contaminated and
sick. I will treat you like a healthy man, like
our old friend Pierre de Craon whom I revere
and love and fear. All that I say is true.

[169]

PIERRE: Thank you, Violaine.

VIOLAINE: Now there is something I have to ask you.

PIERRE: What is it?

VIOLAINE: What is that beautiful story my father told us? What is that *Justitia* you are building at Reims and which is to be more beautiful than Saint-Rémy and Notre-Dame?

PIERRE: It is the church which the tradesmen of Reims gave me to build on the site of the former Parc-aux-Ouilles, there where old Marc-de-l'Evêque was burned last year. First, in order to thank God for seven rich summers when the rest of the kingdom was in distress, wheat and hard fruit, wool, inexpensive and handsome, sheets and parchment sold at a good price to the merchants of Paris and Germany. Second, for the liberties received, the privileges granted by Our Lord the King, the former mandate against us of the bishops Félix II and Abondant de Cramail, annulled by the Pope, all of this by the bare sword and Champagne money. For such is the Christian Republic, not of servile fear, but where each man has his rights, according to whether it is good to establish them, in miraculous diversity, so that charity will be accomplished.

[170]

VIOLAINE: What King are you speaking of and what Pope? For there are two and we don't know which is the good one.

PIERRE: The good one is the one who does us good.

VIOLAINE: That is no way to speak.

PIERRE: Forgive me. I am only an ignorant man.

VIOLAINE: Where does that name come from which you are giving to the new parish?

PIERRE: Didn't you ever hear of Saint Justitia who was martyred in a field of anise at the time of Emperor Julian? Those are the seeds that are put in our gingerbread at the Easter fair. When we were trying to turn aside the water of an underground spring for our foundation, we came upon her tomb with the inscription on a stone broken in two: JUSTITIA ANCILLA DOMINI IN PACE. The small frail skull was broken like a nut. She was a child of eight. And a few of her first teeth were still in her jawbone. Whereupon all of Reims was lost in wonder, and many signs and miracles followed the body which we have placed in the chapel until the work is completed. But we left the small teeth, like seeds, under the great foundation block.

VIOLAINE: What a beautiful story! Our father

told us also that all the ladies of Reims are giving their jewels for the building of Justitia.

PIERRE: We have a great heap of jewels. [*Violaine keeps her eyes lowered and hesitatingly turns a large gold ring which she wears on the fourth finger.*] What is that ring, Violaine?

VIOLAINE: It is a ring that Jacques gave me.
    [*Silence.*]

PIERRE: I congratulate you.
    [*She hands him the ring.*]

VIOLAINE: It's not yet decided. My father has said nothing. Well, that is what I wanted to ask you. Take my beautiful ring which is all I have. Jacques gave it to me in secret.

PIERRE: I don't want it.

VIOLAINE: Take it quickly or I won't be strong enough to give it up.
    [*He takes the ring.*]

PIERRE: What will your fiancé think?

VIOLAINE: He is not exactly my fiancé yet. Giving up the ring won't change my heart. He knows me. He will give me another, of silver. This one was too beautiful for me to wear.

PIERRE [*examining it*]: It is of vegetable gold, like the rings they used to make long ago with an alloy of honey. It is soft as wax and nothing can break it.

[172]

VIOLAINE: Jacques found it in the earth when he was ploughing, in a place where sometimes you can find old swords all turned green and pretty pieces of glass. I was afraid to wear that heathen object which belongs to the dead.

PIERRE: I accept this pure gold.

VIOLAINE: Kiss my sister Justitia for me.

PIERRE [*looking at her suddenly, as if struck by an idea*]: Is that all you have to give me for her, a little gold taken off your finger?

VIOLAINE: Isn't that enough to pay for one small stone?

PIERRE: Justitia is one large stone herself.

VIOLAINE [*laughing*]: I'm not from the same quarry.

PIERRE: The stone needed at the base isn't the same as that needed at the summit.

VIOLAINE: If I am a stone, let me be the one that grinds the grain and that is coupled with the twin grindstone.

PIERRE: Justitia too was only a humble small child close to her mother until the moment God called her to confession.

VIOLAINE: But no one wishes me any harm. Do I have to go to the Saracens and preach the Gospel?

[173]

PIERRE: It is not for the stone to choose its place, but for the Master Artisan who found it.

VIOLAINE: Praise be to God who gave me my place so early. I don't have to look any further. And I don't ask Him for any other place. I am Violaine. I am eighteen. My father's name is Anne Vercors. My mother's is Elizabeth. My sister is called Mara. My fiancé, Jacques. There! That's all. There's nothing more to know. Everything is perfectly clear. Everything is predictable. And I am very happy. I am free. I have nothing to worry about. Someone else will be in charge of me, the poor man, and he knows all that has to be done. Sower of steeples, come to Combernon! We will give you stone and wood, but you will not have the daughter of the house. Besides, isn't this place already the house of God, the land of God, the service of God? Isn't our one duty the nuns of Monsanvierge whom we have to feed and watch over, giving them wine and wax and bread which comes from the half-visible thrashing-floor of angels? Just as the great lords have their pigeon-house, we have ours too, recognizable from a distance.

PIERRE: Once when I was passing through the forest of Fisme, I heard two handsome oak trees speaking to one another, praising God who had made them unshakable in the place where they had been born. Now, on the prow of a boat, one is waging war against the Turks on the Oceanic Sea, and the other, cut by me, props up, in the Tower of Laon, the good bell Jehanne whose voice can be heard ten leagues away. In my profession, young girl, we keep our eyes open. I can recognize good stone under juniper trees and fine wood as easily as a woodpecker can. In the same way I recognize men and women.

VIOLAINE: But not young girls, maître Pierre! They are too delicate for you. And to begin with, there is nothing to know about them.

PIERRE [*half-voice*]: Do you love him very much?

VIOLAINE [*eyes lowered*]: It is a great mystery between us.

PIERRE: Bless you in your pure heart! Holiness doesn't come from being stoned by the Turks or kissing a leper on his mouth, but by keeping the commandment of God, whether it means staying in our own place or mounting higher.

VIOLAINE: How beautiful the universe and how happy I am!

[175]

PIERRE [*half-voice*]: How beautiful the universe and how unhappy I am!

VIOLAINE [*pointing upward*]: You from the city, listen! [*Pause.*] Can you hear way up there a tiny soul that is singing?

PIERRE: It's a lark.

VIOLAINE: It's a lark, alleluia! A lark of Christendom, alleluia, alleluia! Hear it sing four times one after the other and always higher! Do you see it, with wings outstretched, a small vibrant cross, like the seraphim which are only wings, without feet, and a piercing voice before the throne of God?

PIERRE: I hear it. And this is how once I heard it at dawn, on the day we consecrated my daughter, Notre-Dame de la Couture. A bit of gold was shining like a new star at the far tip of that huge thing I had made.

VIOLAINE: Pierre de Craon, if you had had your way with me, would you be more joyful now, or should I be more beautiful?

PIERRE: No, Violaine.

VIOLAINE: Would I still be the same Violaine you loved?

PIERRE: No, not she, but someone else.

VIOLAINE: Which do you prefer, Pierre? That

[176]

I share my joy with you, or that I share your grief?

PIERRE: Sing at high heaven, lark of France!

VIOLAINE: Forgive me if I am too happy, if the man I love, loves me, and I am sure of him, and I know he loves me, and all is peaceful between us. Forgive me if God made me for happiness, and not for evil and suffering.

PIERRE: You mount to heaven in one flight. But I need, just in order to mount a bit, the work of a cathedral and its deep foundation.

VIOLAINE: Tell me that you forgive Jacques because he is going to marry me.

PIERRE: No, I do not forgive him.

VIOLAINE: Hate does you no good, Pierre, and it makes me sorrowful.

PIERRE: Why do you make me talk? Why do you force me to show the terrible wound which isn't to be seen? Let me go and don't ask me anything else. We'll never see one another again. But I am carrying off his ring.

VIOLAINE: Leave your hate here, in place of the ring, and I'll give it back when you need it.

PIERRE: I am an unhappy man, Violaine! It is hard to be a leper and to carry about the infamous sore, to know that you won't be cured and there is no remedy, but that each day it spreads and devours. Hard to be alone and to bear one's own poison and to feel oneself corrupt when still alive. To taste death, not once but ten times, without foregoing any part of the terrible alchemy of the tomb up to the very end. It is you who gave me this sickness, through your beauty, because before seeing you I was pure and joyous. My heart was in my work alone, and I served someone else. And now it's my turn to give orders, and others come to me for the plans. Now you are turning toward me with that smile full of poison!

VIOLAINE: The poison was not in me, Pierre!

PIERRE: I hate it. It was in me and it still is, and this sick flesh has not cured my poisoned soul. Sweet Violaine, was it possible for me to see you without loving you?

VIOLAINE: Was that the way to show your love?

PIERRE: Is it my fault if the fruit holds on to the branch? Where is the man who loves who doesn't want to have all he loves?

VIOLAINE: Is that why you tried to destroy me?

PIERRE: A man outraged has his suffering as well as a woman.

VIOLAINE: In what way did I fail you?

[178]

PIERRE: Image of eternal beauty, you are not mine.

VIOLAINE: I am not an image. That is no way to talk.

PIERRE: In taking you, another man takes what was mine.

VIOLAINE: You still have the image.

PIERRE: Another man takes Violaine from me and leaves me with my contaminated flesh and tormented mind.

VIOLAINE: Be a man, Pierre. Be worthy of the flame consuming you. And if you have to be devoured, let it be on a gold candelabrum, like the Pascal candle in the sanctuary burning for the glory of the Church.

PIERRE: After so many sublime steeple tops, shall I never see the top of my own small house among the trees? So many spires whose shadow as it turns inscribes the hour over the city! Am I never to make the drawing of an oven or of a children's room?

VIOLAINE: I shouldn't have taken for myself alone what belongs to everyone.

PIERRE: Violaine, when is the wedding?

VIOLAINE: At Michelmas, I suppose, when the harvest is in.

PIERRE: On that day, when the bells of Monsan-

[179]

vierge have stopped ringing, listen carefully and you will hear me answering far off from Reims.

VIOLAINE: Who takes care of you there?

PIERRE: I have always lived like a workman. A pellet of hay between two stones is all I need, a leather coat, a little bacon with my bread.

VIOLAINE: Poor Pierre!

PIERRE: Don't pity me for that. I have to live alone. I don't live on a par with other men, I am always under the ground, with the foundation, or in the sky, with a steeple.

VIOLAINE: We couldn't have set up housekeeping together. I am dizzy even if I go up to the hay-loft.

PIERRE: My wife will be this one church which is going to be taken from my side like a stone Eve, in my sleep of suffering. I hope I will soon feel rising up under me my vast work, and place my hand on that indestructible thing which I made and which holds together with all its parts, a self-contained work built with strong stone so that the principle will have its beginning there, a work of mine which God inhabits! I won't come down again. A hundred feet below, on the checkered pavement, a

[180]

group of young girls arm in arm will point me out!

VIOLAINE: You must come down. Who knows whether I won't need you some day?

PIERRE: Farewell, Violaine, my beloved. I shall not see you again.

VIOLAINE: Who knows whether you will never see me again?

PIERRE: Farewell, Violaine! Already I have done many things. Other things remain for me to do and the bringing to life of churches. They are shadows with God. Not the hours of the Office in a book, but the real hours with a cathedral whose sun in its course makes light and shadow on all the parts! I am taking your ring. With this small circle I will make a gold seed. "The Lord poised the earth on the hidden streams," as it is said in the baptismal psalm. I will see that the morning gold has a place between the walls of Justitia. Profane light changes but not the light I will purify under the vaults, like that of the human soul so that the host will remain in the midst, the soul of my child Violaine, in whom my heart takes pleasure. Some churches are like hollow abysses, and others like furnaces, and others of such

[181]

precision, and built with such art that everything is proportionate and fits into place. But the one I am going to build will be under its own shadow like a church of condensed gold and like a pyxidium filled with manna.

VIOLAINE: O Master Pierre, what a beautiful window you gave the monks of Climchy!

PIERRE: Glass-making is not my art, although I know something about it. But before the glass, the architect, by the plan he knows, constructs the apparatus of stone like a filter in the waters of the light of God, and gives to the entire edifice its orient as if to a pearl. [*Mara Vercors has come in and watches without their seeing her.*] And now, farewell! The sun is up. I should be far on my way already.

VIOLAINE: Goodby, Pierre!

PIERRE: Goodby, Violaine!

VIOLAINE: Poor Pierre!

[*She looks at him, her eyes full of tears, hesitates, and holds out her hand. He takes it and while he holds it in his, she leans over and kisses him on the face. Mara shows surprise and leaves. Pierre de Craon and Violaine leave in opposite directions.*]

ACT I

SCENE I

The kitchen at Combernon, a vast room with a large fireplace bearing an emblazoned basket, a long table in the middle and all utensils, as in a painting of Breughel. The Mother, in front of the fireplace, is stirring the embers. Anne Vercors, standing, watches her. He is a tall strong man of sixty, with a large blond beard mixed with a good deal of white.

THE MOTHER [*without turning*]: Why are you looking at me that way?

ANNE VERCORS [*thinking*]: The end is already here. It's like a picture book when you're about to turn the last page. "After the night, when the wife had stirred the hearth fire . . ." and the simple story ends. It is as if already I was no longer here. There before my eyes, I am already seeing her as if she were a memory. [*Out loud.*] Since the time we were wed with the ring which marked the consent, each day of each month had been a year. For a long time you remained useless to me like a tree which produces only a shadow. Then one day, Elizabeth, we looked at one another in the midway of our life. I kissed the first lines on your brow and around your eyes. And as on the day of our wedding, we embraced and possessed one another, not in joy, but in the tenderness and compassion and pity of our faith. And behold there was a child with us and the uprightness of the sweet narcissus, Violaine. And then the second was born, Mara, who was dark. A second girl, and there was no boy. [*Pause.*] Come, now, say what you have to say, for I know when it is when you begin to speak without looking, saying something and nothing. Speak!

MOTHER: You know that no one can talk to you. You are never here, and I have to catch you to sew on a button. You don't hear us. You're like a watch-dog, listening to sounds at the door. Men have no understanding.

ANNE: Now the little girls have grown up.

MOTHER: No, they haven't.

ANNE: What husbands are we going to get for them?

MOTHER: Husbands, Anne? There's time to think about that.

ANNE: How devious a woman is! Whenever you think one thing, you begin by saying its opposite. But I know you well, sly woman that you are.

MOTHER: I have no more to say.

ANNE: Jacques Hury.

[186]

MOTHER: What about him?

ANNE: I am going to give him Violaine. He will take the place of the boy I never had. He's a good courageous man. I have known him since he was a small boy when his mother gave him to us. I've taught him all he knows about wheat, animals, people, weapons, tools, the weather, the habits of this ancient soil, the way to reflect before answering. I have seen him grow into a man while he was watching me, and I've seen his first beard grow on his open face, straight, in brushes like ears of barley. He isn't one to contradict you, but he thinks deeply like the soil accepting all the seeds. What is false, since it makes no roots, dies; and so for what is true, you can't say he believes in it, but it grows in him, having found nourishment.

MOTHER: How do you know whether they love one another?

ANNE: Violaine will do what I ask. As for him, I know he loves her and you know it too. But the fool doesn't dare speak to me about it. I will give her to him if that is what he wants. That is the way it will be.

MOTHER: Perhaps it is best that way.

ANNE: Have you nothing more to say?

MOTHER: What do you mean?

ANNE: Well, I'm going to have him come here.

MOTHER: Have him come here? Anne!

ANNE: Everything has to be put in order now. I'll tell you why very soon.

MOTHER: Why are you speaking this way? Anne, listen to me. I'm afraid . . .

ANNE: Afraid of what?

MOTHER: Mara slept in my room this winter when you were sick and we used to talk at night in our beds. I know that he's a good boy and I love him almost as if he were my son. It is true he has no fortune, but he works well in the fields and he comes from a good family. We could give them our rent from the Demi-Muids and the low farmlands which are too far away for us.—I had meant to speak to you about him.

ANNE: What is on your mind?

MOTHER: There is no point in speaking now. Violaine is the elder.

ANNE: Come, speak up.

MOTHER: How do you know for sure that he loves her? Our friend maître Pierre—I wonder why he stayed by himself this time and saw no one?—you saw him last year when he came. He looked at her when she waited on us. He

has no land, but he earns a lot of money. And
while he spoke, do you remember how she
listened to him, her eyes wide open like some
simpleton forgetting to pour the wine, so that
I lost my temper! And Mara! You know how
stubborn she is! If she gets the idea into her
head to marry Jacques, she won't give up
easily. I don't know. Perhaps it is better to . . .

ANNE: What is all this foolishness?

MOTHER: We can talk, can't we? We don't
have to lose our temper.

ANNE: This I want. Jacques will marry Violaine.

MOTHER: So be it. Let him marry her!

ANNE: And now there is something else I have
to say. I'm leaving.

MOTHER: Leaving? You say you're leaving?

ANNE: That is why Jacques has to marry Violaine without delay and be the man here in my
place.

MOTHER: You're leaving? for good? And where
are you going?

ANNE [*pointing south*]: In that direction.

MOTHER: To Château?

ANNE: Farther than Château.

MOTHER [*lowering her voice*]: To Bourges,
where the other king is?

ANNE: I am going to Jerusalem, where the King of Kings is.

MOTHER: Good Lord! [*She sits down.*] Isn't this country good enough for you?

ANNE: There is too much suffering in France.

MOTHER: But we're safe here and no one comes near Reims.

ANNE: That's the point.

MOTHER: What do you mean?

ANNE: That's the point. We're too happy. And others aren't happy enough.

MOTHER: It is no fault of ours, Anne.

ANNE: Neither is it theirs.

MOTHER: All that I know is that you are here and I have two children.

ANNE: But at least you can see that everything is troubled and out of place, and everyone is bewildered and trying to find where his place is. The smoke we sometimes see in the distance doesn't come from useless straw that is burning. And what about the hordes of poor people who come from every direction? There is no longer any king in France, as was prophesied by the prophet.

MOTHER: Is that what you were reading to us a few days ago?

ANNE: Instead of a king, we have two children.

One, an Englishman, on his island, and the other, so small you can't see him, among the reeds of the Loire. Instead of the Pope, we have three popes, and instead of Rome, there is some council or other in Switzerland. Since nothing is held in place by a weight from above, there is conflict and movement everywhere.

MOTHER: And now you too want to move about.

ANNE: I can't stay here any longer.

MOTHER: Anne, have I ever hurt you in any way?

ANNE: No, Elizabeth.

MOTHER: And now you are leaving me in my old age.

ANNE: You yourself will give me leave.

MOTHER: Your love for me is over and you are not happy with me.

ANNE: I am tired of being happy.

MOTHER: Don't scorn the gift of happiness which comes from God.

ANNE: Praise be to God who has showered His blessings on me! Thirty years ago I received this sacred fief from my father and for thirty years God's rain has fallen on my fields. For ten years every hour of work He has paid me four times over and even five, as if He didn't wish to leave any balance between us and any account open. Everything else perishes and I am spared. In such a way that I shall appear before Him empty and without a title, in the company of those who have received their reward.

MOTHER: The gratitude of your heart will be sufficient.

ANNE: My hunger for the gifts of God is not appeased. Because I have received these gifts, should I leave to others the greater gifts?

MOTHER: I don't understand you.

ANNE: Which can receive more, an empty vase or a full one? Which needs more water, the cistern or the spring?

MOTHER: The long summer has almost dried up our cistern.

ANNE: Such is the evil of the world that each man wants to enjoy his blessings as if they had been created for him, and not as if he had received them from God as a duty, the Lord his fief, the father his children, the king his kingdom and the cleric his title. That is why God caused to pass from Him all things which pass, and sent to each man freedom and fasting.

Why shouldn't the heritage of others be mine
also?

MOTHER: Your duty is with us.

ANNE: Not if you release me from it.

MOTHER: I shall not release you.

ANNE: Can't you see that what I had to do is
done. The two children have grown up.
Jacques is here and taking my place.

MOTHER: Who calls you to such a distance?

ANNE [smiles]: An angel blowing the trumpet.

MOTHER: What trumpet?

ANNE: The trumpet with no sound which everyone hears. The trumpet which at times calls out
every man so that the parts may be redis-
tributed. Jehosaphat's before it sounded. Bethlehem's when Augustus counted the earth. The
trumpet of the Ascension when the Apostles
were called together. The voice replacing the
Word when the leader can no longer be heard
by the body seeking its unity.

MOTHER: Jerusalem is so far!

ANNE: Paradise is still farther.

MOTHER: God is with us even here, in His
tabernacle.

ANNE: But He's not in the hole in the earth.

MOTHER: What hole?

[193]

ANNE: The one made by the Cross when it was planted. The Cross draws everything to Itself. It is the point that cannot be dissolved, the nodus that cannot be broken, the common patrimony, the inner landmark which cannot be pulled up, the center and the umbilicus of the earth, the mid-point of humanity where everything is held together.

MOTHER: What can one pilgrim do?

ANNE: I am not alone. A great people rejoices and departs with me. The assembly of all my dead with me, the souls one on the other of which only the stone remains, all those stones baptized with me which are calling for their foundation! And because it is true that the Christian is not alone but is in communion with all his brothers, the entire kingdom with me calls and pulls on the throne of God, and finds in relation with it a sense of direction. I am their deputy and carry them with me to attach them again to the eternal leader.

MOTHER: How do you know that we won't need you here?

ANNE: How do you know that I am not needed in some other place? Everything is in motion. How do you know that I am not disturbing the

[194]

order of God by staying here where need of me no longer exists?

MOTHER: I know your will is inflexible.

ANNE [*tenderly, changing his voice*]: You are still young and beautiful to me. And great is the love I have for my sweet Elizabeth with her black hair.

MOTHER: My hair is gray.

ANNE: Say I can go, Elizabeth . . .

MOTHER: For thirty years you never left me once. What will become of me without my master and my companion?

ANNE: Give at this moment in a low voice the consent for this separation which long ago you said in a full voice and which united us.
     [*Silence.*]

MOTHER [*low voice*]: I give my consent, Anne.

ANNE: Patience, Bess! In a short time I shall be back. Can't you have faith in me, for a little while, when I am not here? There will soon be another separation. Come, put some food in a bag that will last me two days. I must leave.

MOTHER: You are going today?

ANNE: Yes, today. [*She bows her head and doesn't move. He embraces her and she still doesn't move.*] Farewell, Elizabeth!

MOTHER: You are old and I shall never see you again.

ANNE: Now I must get Jacques.
   [*He leaves.*]

SCENE II

MARA: Go to him and say that she must not marry him.

MOTHER: Were you here, Mara?

MARA: I tell you, go and say that she can't marry him.

MOTHER: Who are you talking about? How do you know whether she is to marry him?

MARA: I was here. I heard everything.

MOTHER: Then you know it's your father who wants this. You saw that I did what I could, but you can't make him change his mind.

MARA: Go to him and say that she can't marry him, or I'll kill myself.

MOTHER: Mara!

MARA: I'll hang myself in the woodshed, there where you found the cat strung up.

MOTHER: Mara, that is evil!

MARA: She is going to take him away from me. I should be his wife and not her. She knows very well that it should be me.

[196]

MOTHER: She is the elder.

MARA: What difference does that make?

MOTHER: It's the will of your father.

MARA: I don't care about that.

MOTHER: Jacques Hury loves her.

MARA: That is not true! Oh! I know that you don't love me. You have always preferred her. When you speak of your Violaine, it is all sweetness. Like a cherry you're eating just at the moment you spit out the stone.

But Mara is a chattering magpie, hard as nails, bitter as a wild cherry.

Ah! but your Violaine has beauty. And she will inherit Combernon. What can that little fool do? Can she drive the cart like me? She thinks she's one of the saints in glory. Well, I am Mara Vercors and I can't stand injustice and deception. I speak the truth and that makes people mad. Let them get mad! I'll spit in their faces. Every one of those stupid women gets out of my way.

Now everything is for her and nothing for me.

MOTHER: You will have your share.

MARA: I know what that will be. The sand banks on the hill. The clay fields where you need five oxen for the ploughing. The poor lands of Chinchy.

MOTHER: Crops grow there just the same.

MARA: Yes! Doggrass and foxtail, senna and mullein. Things I can make an infusion with.

MOTHER: You're wicked to say these things that are not true. You know you won't be cheated out of anything. But you have always been bad. When you were small, you never cried when you were whipped. Isn't she the older? Why are you so jealous? She has never done you any harm, but always did what you asked. She is to be married the first, and then your turn will come next. Anyway, it's too late. Your father is leaving and my heart is too heavy to talk with you. He is speaking to Violaine and he is going to call Jacques in.

MARA: Yes, I know. Go to him right away. Go!

MOTHER: Go where?

MARA: You know it's my place. Tell me, mother, that she can't marry him.

MOTHER: I will do nothing of the kind.

MARA: Just tell him what I've told you. Tell him that I'll kill myself. Do you understand what I'm saying?

MOTHER: Ha!

MARA: You don't think I'll do it?

[198]

MOTHER: Yes, I think you would.

MARA: Well, go!

MOTHER: You're a wicked girl.

MARA: There's no blame for you in this. Just tell him what I said.

MOTHER: How do you know that he wants to marry you?

MARA: I am sure he doesn't.

MOTHER: Well, don't think that I'm going to urge Violaine to do what you want. I'll only repeat what you said. If she follows my advice, she won't be foolish enough to give in to you.
[*She leaves.*]

SCENE III

[*Enter Anne Vercors and Jacques Hury, then Violaine and servants of the farm.*]

ANNE [*stopping*]: Is what you're telling me true?

JACQUES: I swear it! This time I caught him in the act, with the pruning-hook in his hand. I had quietly come up behind him and then I jumped on him with my whole weight and body as you jump on a hare in its burrow at harvest time. At his side there were twenty young poplar trees tied together, the ones you like the best.

ANNE: Why didn't he come to me? I would have given him the wood he needed.

JACQUES: The wood he needs is the handle of my whip. It's not a question of need, it's malice, it's the will to be mean. They are like that in Chevoche, people always ready to do anything for notoriety, just to defy you. I'd like to cut off that man's ears with my knife.

ANNE: No.

JACQUES: At least let me tie him to the portcullis by his wrists in front of the main gate, with his face turned toward the spikes and the dog Faraud to keep guard.

ANNE: Not that either.

JACQUES: What do you want me to do?

ANNE: Send him home.

JACQUES: With his bundle of trees?

ANNE: To which I will add more trees.

JACQUES: This is unwise, master.

ANNE: Be sure to tie them in the middle so he won't lose them. It will be easier for him to cross the ford of Saponay.

JACQUES: But shouldn't a man defend his own rights?

ANNE: Yes, Jacques, what I'm doing is wrong. But I'm cowardly and old, and I'm tired of fighting and defending my rights. Once I was

L'ANNONCE FAITE À MARIE, *Setting for the Prologue. Théâtre de l'Athénée.*

Alain Cuny as Pierre de Craon and Hélène Sauvaneix as Violaine in L'AN-NONCE FAITE À MARIE, *Prologue.* Théâtre Hébertot.

Louis Jouvet as Anne in L'ANNONCE FAITE À MARIE, *Act I. Théâtre de l'Athénée.*

Presse Be

Monique Mélinand in Act II, scene 5,
L'ANNONCE FAITE À MARIE. *Théâtre de
l'Athénée.*

Presse Bernand

Final scene Act II, L'ANNONCE FAITE À MARIE. *Théâtre de l'Athénée.*

Act III, scene 3, Violaine and Mara, L'AN-
NONCE FAITE À MARIE. *Théâtre de l'Athénée.*

Louis Jouvet as Anne and Monique Mé-linand as Violaine in Act IV, scene 3, L'ANNONCE FAITE À MARIE. *Théâtre de l'Athénée.*

Presse Bernand

Concluding scene, L'ANNONCE FAITE À MARIE. *Théâtre Hébertot.*

as harsh as you are now. There is a time to take
all that is due a man, and there is another time
to give it up. The flowering tree has to be protected, but when the tree is laden with fruit,
let everyone come and help himself. I pray to
be unjust on few occasions, so that God will
be literally unjust with me. Moreover, from
now on you will do as you want, because
Combernon will be in your charge.

JACQUES: What are you saying?

MOTHER: He is going to Jerusalem as a pilgrim.

JACQUES: Jerusalem!

ANNE: Yes, I'm leaving now.

JACQUES: I don't understand. What does this
mean?

ANNE: You heard what she said.

JACQUES: You leave us just like that, at the time
of the heaviest work?

ANNE: Combernon doesn't need two masters.

JACQUES: But I am only a kind of son for you.

ANNE: You will take my place as the father.

JACQUES: I don't understand.

ANNE: I am going away. I am giving Combernon
to you. As my father gave it to me, and his
father to him, as Saint Rémy of Reims gave it
to Rudolph the Frank, the first of our lineage.
As Geneviève of Paris gave it to Saint Rémy

[201]

who owned this land which was then pagan, congested with poor trees and self-sown briars. With the sword and fire Rudolph made it into Christian land and exposed it bare and broken to the waters of baptism. Both field and hill they covered with even furrows, just as an industrious monk makes a copy line by line of the word of God. And they founded Monsanvierge on the mountain, where Satan had been honored. At first it was only a hut made of logs and reeds whose door was sealed up by the bishop, and two nuns kept watch. And Combernon at the foot of the mountain, a richly supplied house. So this land is free which we inherit from Saint Rémy in heaven, and we pay our tithe high up on the crest to that flight of doves which take cover for a moment to sing their lamentations. Everything exists within God. For those who live in God the fruit of their work does not cease. It passes and returns to us in its time, in the splendor of its succession, as the great clouds on the way to Germany pass over the summer harvests all day long. The animals here are never sick. Udders and wells never dry up. The wheat is hard as gold and the straw is as firm as iron. Against plunderers we have weapons and the walls of

Combernon and our neighbor the king. Reap
the harvest which I have sown, as once I myself turned over the turf on the furrow which
my father had ploughed. The work of the
farmer is good. The sun is our shining ox and
the rain our banker, and every day on the
fields God is our companion, doing the best He
can with all of us. Others receive their fortune
from men but we receive ours straight from
heaven itself, a hundred for one, a stalk of
grain for a seed and a tree for a kernel. Such is
the justice of God for us, such is the measure
with which He repays us. The earth needs the
sky, the body needs the spirit, all things created
by Him are in communion, all at all times are
necessary to one another. Take hold of the
handles of the plough in my place, deliver the
earth of that bread which God Himself desired.
Feed all creatures, men and animals, spirits and
bodies and immortal souls. You women and
servants are my witnesses. Here is the son of
my choice, Jacques Hury. I am leaving and he
will stay in my place. Obey him.

JACQUES: May your will be done.

ANNE: Violaine, you who were born the first in
the place of the son I did not have, you have
inherited my name and in you I shall be given

[203]

to someone else. Violaine, when you have a husband, do not scorn the love of your father. For you cannot give to your father what he gave you, even if you wished to. There is equality between husband and wife. What they do not know, they accept on faith one from the other. This is their mutual love of God and the servitude by which the woman's breast swells with milk. The father sees his children outside of himself and knows what was placed within him. My daughter, know your father! The love of the Heavenly Father asks no return and the child has no need to earn it or deserve it. It was with him before the beginning and it remains his fortune, his inheritance, his recourse, his honor, his title, his justification. My soul is not separate from the soul I gave to you. What I gave cannot be returned. Know that I am your father. That is all I ask. No male child came from me. All that I put into the world is a woman, that in me which gives and is given is a woman. And now the time has come to separate.

VIOLAINE: Father, don't say that. It is cruel.

ANNE: Jacques, you are the man for whom I have love. Take her. I give you my daughter Violaine. Take my name from her. Love her,

[204]

for she is precious as gold, every day of your life, like the bread we need every day. She is simple and obedient. She is full of feeling and secretive. Do her no harm and treat her tenderly. Everything here is yours except the share which will be given to Mara as I have planned.

JACQUES: Are you giving your daughter and your fortune?

ANNE: I am giving you everything at once in as much as they are mine.

JACQUES: But who can tell whether she wants me?

ANNE: Yes, who can tell?

[*Violaine looks at Jacques and says yes without speaking.*]

JACQUES: Will you have me, Violaine?

VIOLAINE: It is the wish of my father.

JACQUES: Is it yours also?

VIOLAINE: It is mine also.

JACQUES: Violaine, how do I go about asking you?

VIOLAINE: You must hurry up. There is not too much time.

JACQUES: I take you, then, before the eyes of God, and I will not let you go. [*He takes both her hands.*] I really have you now, your hand

[205]

and your arm and all that your arm is attached
to. Anne and Elizabeth, your daughter is no
longer yours. She belongs only to me.

ANNE: There now, they are married. It is over.
How does the mother feel?

MOTHER: I am very happy.

[*She cries.*]

ANNE: Like a woman, she is crying. Our children
are taken and we are left alone. An old woman
who keeps alive on a bit of milk and a small
piece of cake, and an old man whose ears are
full of white hairs like the heart of an artichoke.
—You must get the wedding gown ready. I
will not be here at your wedding.

VIOLAINE: What, father?

MOTHER: Anne!

ANNE: I am leaving now.

VIOLAINE: Oh father! before we are married?

ANNE: I have to. Your mother will explain everything.

[*Mara enters.*]

MOTHER: How long a time will you stay there?

ANNE: I don't know. Perhaps a very short time.
I shall be back soon.

[*Silence.*]

VOICE OF A CHILD [*in the distance*]:

Oriole, oriole,

Who eats the cherry and leaves the stone!

ANNE: The oriole is whistling in the rose golden tree. What does it say? that the rain last night was like gold for the earth after the long days of summer heat. What does it say? that it is good to plough the land. What does it say now? that the air has cleared, that God is good, that there are two more hours before noon. What does the little bird say now? That it is time for the old man to go off to some other place and let everyone go back to work.— Jacques, I leave you my possessions. Protect these women.

JACQUES: Are you really leaving?

ANNE: Haven't you heard what I've been saying?

JACQUES: But leaving like this, right away?

ANNE: The time has come.

MOTHER: You won't leave before eating?

> [*The servants have been preparing the large table for the meal.*]

ANNE [*to a servant*]: Get my bag and my hat. Bring my shoes and my cloak. I haven't the time to eat this meal with you.

MOTHER: Anne, how long a time will you stay there? One year, two years? More than two years?

[207]

ANNE: Yes, one or two years. Put my shoes on for me. [*The Mother kneels and puts the shoes on his feet.*] For the first time I'm leaving this house, and this estate of Combernon. Watch over everything. Jacques will be here in my place. Here is the fireplace where there must always be a fire, and here is the big table where there's a place for everyone. Take your places. For the last time I will break bread with you. [*He sits at the head of the table, the Mother on his right. The men and women servants stand, at their places. He takes the bread, makes the sign of the cross on it with his knife, cuts it and has Violaine and Mara pass it out. He keeps the last piece. Then he solemnly turns to the Mother and opens his arms.*] Farewell, Elizabeth!

MOTHER [*weeping, in his arms*]: You will not see me again.

ANNE [*lower voice*]: Farewell, Elizabeth. [*He turns toward Mara and looks at her solemnly for a long time, then holds out his hand.*] Farewell, Mara! Be good!

MARA [*kissing his hand*]: Goodby, father!
　　　　[*Silence. Anne Vercors is standing and looking ahead of him, as if he didn't see Violaine who, worried, stands beside*

[208]

him. At the end, he turns a bit toward her and she throws her arms around his neck and sobs, her face on his chest.]

ANNE [*to the servants, as if he didn't see them*]: Farewell to all of you! I have always been fair to you. If anyone says I haven't, he lies. I am not like other masters. When something is well done, I say so, and I criticize when there is need. Now I am leaving and you must behave as if I were here. For I will return. I shall return at a time when you don't expect me. [*He shakes hands with them.*] Have someone bring my horse. [*Silence. Leaning toward Violaine who still embraces him.*] What is the matter, my child? You have now a husband in place of a father.

VIOLAINE: Oh father! father!

[*Gently he takes her arms from his neck.*]

MOTHER: Tell us when you'll come back.

ANNE: I can't tell you. Perhaps it will be in the morning. Or perhaps at noon when you are eating. Or perhaps at night, when you wake up, you will hear my footstep. Farewell!

[*He leaves.*]

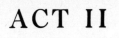

ACT II

Two weeks later. The beginning of July. Noon.
A large orchard symmetrically planted with
round trees. Up stage, and a bit to the side, walls
and towers, and the long buildings, with tile roof,
of Combernon. Then the side of an abrupt hill
which rises up. High up the gigantic stone arch
of Monsanvierge without an opening and its five
towers like the cathedral of Laon, and the large
white wound in its side, the opening through
which the Queen Mother of France has just
passed. Everything vibrates in the full sunlight.

VOICE OF WOMAN HIGH UP [*from the highest*
tower of Monsanvierge]:
Salve Regina mater misericordiae
Vita dulcedo et spes nostra salve
Ad te clamamus exules filii Hevae
Ad te suspiramus gementes et flentes in hac
lacrymarum valle.
Eia ergo advocata nostra illos tuos misericordes
oculos ad nos converte
Et Jesum benedictum fructum ventris tui nobis
post hoc exilium ostende
O clemens
O pia
O dulcis Virgo Maria
[*Long pause.*]
[213]

SCENE I

[Enter Mother and Mara]

MARA: What did she say?

MOTHER: As we walked I brought up the subject. These last few days she has lost her good spirits.

MARA: She is talking all the time.

MOTHER: But she never laughs. It makes me sad. Perhaps it is because Jacquin isn't here. But he comes back today. And also her father went away.

MARA: Is that all you said to her?

MOTHER: That's what I said, and the rest too without changing anything, exactly as you had me recite it. Jacquin and you, that you love him, and all the rest, and that this time she mustn't be a fool and let herself be led. I added that and repeated it two or three times. How can a marriage, which is practically made, be broken, against the father's will? What will people think?

MARA: What answer did she give?

MOTHER: She began to laugh and I began to weep.

MARA: I'll make her laugh.

[214]

MOTHER: But it wasn't the kind of laughter I like in her, and so I began to cry. I said, "no, no, Violaine, my child!" But without speaking, she made a sign with her hand that she wanted to be alone. Ah! the trouble there is with bringing up children!

MARA: Shuh!

MOTHER: What's the matter? I'm sorry about what I've done.

MARA: She's over there, at the end of the field, walking behind the trees. You can't see her now.

> [*Silence. From backstage the sound of a horn.*]

MOTHER: It's Jacques coming home. I know the sound of his horn.

MARA: Let's move away from here.

> [*They leave.*]

SCENE II

> [*Enter Jacques Hury.*]

JACQUES [*looking around*]: I don't see her. And yet she sent me word she wanted to see me here this first morning. [*Enter Mara. She approaches Jacques and at six feet away makes a deep curtsy.*] Good morning, Mara!

[215]

MARA: Your servant, my lord!

JACQUES: What's this behavior?

MARA: I am paying homage. Aren't you the master here, dependent only on God, like the King of France himself and Emperor Charlemagne?

JACQUES: Make fun, if you wish, but it is true. Dear Sister Mara, it is a miracle and I am full of joy.

MARA: I am not your *dear sister!* I am your servant, since I have to be. Man from Braine, son of a serf, I am not your sister and you are not of our blood.

JACQUES: I am the husband of Violaine.

MARA: You aren't yet.

JACQUES: I will be tomorrow.

MARA: Who can tell?

JACQUES: Mara, I have thought a great deal about that story you told me the other day. You must have dreamt it.

MARA: What story?

JACQUES: Don't pretend to be surprised. The story of the stone mason, and the secret kiss at daybreak.

MARA: That may be. Perhaps I didn't see too well. Yet I have good eyesight.

JACQUES: I have been told confidentially the man is a leper.

MARA: I don't love you, Jacques. But you have
the right to know everything. Everything must
be clear and open at Monsanvierge which is a
monstrance over the whole kingdom.

JACQUES: It will be all cleared up this morning.

MARA: You are clever and nothing escapes you.

JACQUES: At least I see you don't love me.

MARA: Oh! what did I say and why did I say it?

JACQUES: People here don't think as you do.

MARA: Are you speaking of Violaine? I blush
for her. It is shameful to give herself soul and
body, inside and out.

JACQUES: I know that she's completely mine.

MARA: Yes, how well you speak and how sure
you are of what you own. We own only what
we have made or taken or won.

JACQUES: I like you, Mara, and I have nothing
against you.

MARA: In the same way that you like everything
here, I imagine.

JACQUES: It is not my fault that you are not a
man and that I have taken your fortune.

MARA: How proud and happy you are! Look at
yourself! You can hardly keep from laughing.
You had better laugh or you'll hurt yourself.
[*He laughs.*] I know all the expressions on your
face, Jacques.

[217]

JACQUES: You're mad because you can't upset me.

MARA: The other day when my father was speaking, you laughed with one eye and wept dry tears with the other.

JACQUES: I'm the master of a rich estate.

MARA: My father was old, wasn't he? And you know a few more things than he did.

JACQUES: Each man comes into his own.

MARA: Jacques, you are a handsome man, and now you are turning red.

JACQUES: Stop tormenting me.

MARA: All the same, it's a great pity.

JACQUES: What is a great pity?

MARA: Goodby, husband of Violaine! Goodby, master of Monsanvierge!

JACQUES: I'll prove to you that I am.

MARA: Well then, learn the spirit of this place, man of Braine! Like a peasant you think that everything belongs to you, but you're going to learn that the opposite is true. You're like a peasant who thinks he owns the highest things when he's in the middle of his flat little field. Monsanvierge belongs to God and the master of Monsanvierge is a man of God who himself owns nothing because he holds everything for someone else. That is the lesson we learn here

[218]

from father to child. There is no loftier place than ours. Learn the spirit of your masters, farmer-boy! [*Starts to go out.*] Oh! I met Violaine who gave me a message for you.

JACQUES: Why didn't you tell me earlier?

MARA: She is waiting for you near the fountain.

SCENE III

The fountain of Adoue. A large square hole in a vertical wall of limestone. A thin stream of water comes out with a sad sound. Hanging on the wall are straw crosses and bunches of dried flowers, ex-voto. Thick trees and rose bushes form around the fountain a cradle whose many flowers stand out against the green.

JACQUES [*watching Violaine coming along the winding path. Her dress sparkles in the sunlight as it comes through the leaves.*] Greetings to my fiancée through the flowering branches! [*Violaine enters and stands before him. She is wearing a linen dress and a kind of dalmatic of gold cloth decorated with large red and blue flowers. On her head is a kind of diadem of enamel and silver-plate.*] How beautiful you are, Violaine!

[219]

VIOLAINE: Hello, Jacques! You've been away for so long!

JACQUES: I had to release and sell everything, and free myself in order to be the man of Monsanvierge and your husband.—What is this marvellous costume?

VIOLAINE: I put it on for you. I told you about it once. Don't you recognize it? It's the habit of the recluse nuns of Monsanvierge, almost, that is, without the maniple. The costume they wear in the choir. The dalmatic of the deacon they have the privilege of wearing, since it is something of the priest, and they themselves are hosts. The women of Combernon have the right to wear it twice: on the day of their betrothal, and on the day of their death.

JACQUES: It's true, then, this is the day of our betrothal, Violaine?

VIOLAINE: There is still time, Jacques, we are not yet married. If all you wanted was to please my father, there is still time to reconsider. It is between us now. I will bear you no ill feeling, for as yet there are no promises between us and I don't know if I please you.

JACQUES: How beautiful you are, Violaine! And how beautiful is this world in which you are the blessing which has been kept for me!

[220]

VIOLAINE: It is you, Jacques, who are the best the world has to offer.

JACQUES: Is it true that you are willing to be mine?

VIOLAINE: Yes, it is so, my beloved, I am yours.

JACQUES: Violaine, I greet you as my wife. Sweet Violaine!

VIOLAINE: These are good things to hear, Jacques.

JACQUES: You must never not be here. Swear to me you will never not be the same woman, the same angel who is sent to me.

VIOLAINE: I swear that what is mine will never cease being yours.

JACQUES: As for me, Violaine . . .

VIOLAINE: Say nothing. I ask nothing. You are here and that is all I need. I greet you, Jacques. There is such beauty in this hour that I can ask for nothing else.

JACQUES: Tomorrow will be still more beautiful.

VIOLAINE: Tomorrow I shall have taken off this magnificent robe.

JACQUES: But you will be so close to me that I shan't be able to see you.

VIOLAINE: Yes, very close to you.

JACQUES: You have found your place. How

lonely this garden is and how secretly I am here with you!

VIOLAINE [*low voice*]: Your heart is all I need. I am with you. Don't say anything more.

JACQUES: But tomorrow, before everyone, I shall take my Queen in my arms.

VIOLAINE: Take her and don't let her go. Take me with you so that no one will find me again and do me any harm.

JACQUES: Tell me that at that moment you will not miss the linen and the gold.

VIOLAINE: Was I wrong to make myself beautiful for one small hour?

JACQUES: No. I can't keep from looking at you in your glory.

VIOLAINE: Oh Jacques! tell me once again that I am beautiful.

JACQUES: Yes, Violaine!

VIOLAINE: The most beautiful of all women, and the others are nothing for you?

JACQUES: Yes, Violaine!

VIOLAINE: And you love me as the most loving husband loves the poor creature who has given herself to him?

JACQUES: Yes, Violaine.

VIOLAINE: Who gives herself with all her heart and holds nothing back.

[222]

JACQUES: Don't you believe me, Violaine?

VIOLAINE: I believe you, Jacques. I believe in you. I have trust in you, my beloved.

JACQUES: Then why do you seem so worried and terrified? Show me your left hand. [*She shows it.*] Where is my ring?

VIOLAINE: I will explain all that in a little while and you will be satisfied.

JACQUES: I am, Violaine. I have faith in you.

VIOLAINE: I am more than a ring, Jacques. I am a great treasure.

JACQUES: Yes, Violaine.

VIOLAINE: If I give myself to you, will you be able to protect me who love you?

JACQUES: There you are again, doubting me.

VIOLAINE: After all, I do no wrong in loving you. It is God's will and my father's. I have been entrusted to you. But who knows whether you will be able to defend and protect me? It is enough that I give myself to you completely. The rest is your concern and not mine.

JACQUES: So you have given yourself to me, my wife standing there in the sunlight?

VIOLAINE: Yes, Jacques.

JACQUES: Who then can take you from my arms?

[223]

VIOLAINE: How big the world is and how alone we are!

JACQUES: Poor child! I know how you feel about your father going away. I too feel there is no one here to tell me what to do and what is good or bad. You must help me, Violaine, because I love you.

VIOLAINE: My father left me.

JACQUES: But I am with you, Violaine.

VIOLAINE: My mother has no love for me, nor my sister, although I have done them no harm. All I have is you and I don't know you. [*He makes a move to take her in his arms. She quickly pushes him away.*] Don't touch me, Jacques.

JACQUES: Do you think I'm a leper?

VIOLAINE: Jacques, I have to speak to you, and it is not easy. Don't fail me. I have only you.

JACQUES: No one wishes you any harm.

VIOLAINE: You must know what you are doing when you take me as a wife. Let me speak to you very humbly, my lord Jacques, who are going to receive my soul and my body as your charge from the hands of God and my father who made them. Know that the dowry I bring you is not that of other women, but this holy mountain which prays day and night before

[224]

God, like an altar with incense always mounting, and the lamp always lighted which it is our duty to keep filled with oil. At our marriage there is no witness save that Lord from whom we hold the fief who is the Almighty, the God of Hosts. It is not the July sun which gives us light but His face. Holy things are for those who are holy. Who knows if my heart is pure? Up until now there had always been a male in our race, the sacred charge had always been handed down from father to son, and now for the first time it falls into the hands of a woman and with her becomes the object of covetousness.

JACQUES: Violaine, I am not a cleric or a monk or a saint. I am not the porter or the lay brother of Monsanvierge. I have the charge, and I shall fulfill it, of feeding those nuns who read their prayers together, and filling the basket they send down from heaven each morning. This is the order. I will carry it out. I clearly understand this. It is on my mind, but you mustn't ask anything more. You mustn't ask me to understand what's beyond me and why these holy women are walled up in their pigeon-house. Heaven is for the heavenly and the earth is for those of the earth. Wheat

[225]

doesn't grow by itself and the one in charge needs a good ploughman. Without boasting, I can say I am that man, and no one is my master in that, not even your father. He was old and attached to his ideas. Each man comes in his time and place, and that is justice. When your father gave you to me with Monsanvierge, he knew what he was doing and it was just.

VIOLAINE: But Jacques, I do not love you because it is just. And even if it were not, I would still love you and even more.

JACQUES: I don't understand you, Violaine.

VIOLAINE: Don't force me to speak. You love me and I can only do you harm. Leave me! There can be no justice between us. Only faith and charity. Leave me when there is still time.

JACQUES: I don't understand, Violaine.

VIOLAINE: Beloved, don't force me to tell you my great secret.

JACQUES: What great secret?

VIOLAINE: So great a secret that everything is consummated within it. You will no longer ask to marry me.

JACQUES: I don't understand.

VIOLAINE: Isn't it enough for me to be beautiful at this moment, Jacques? Why ask any-

[226]

thing else? You ask that a flower be beautiful
and sweet-smelling for one moment, and then
it is over. The flower dies but the joy it gave
is not one of those things which have a beginning or an end. Am I not pretty enough? What
more do you need? I can see your eyes, dear
Jacques. Is there anything in you at this moment which does not love me and which doubts
me? Isn't my soul enough? Take it and I will
still be here. Inhale it deep within you. Only
a moment is needed for dying, and death itself,
the death of one of us in the other, will not
extinguish us more than love. Is there any need
to live when we are dead? What more is there
to do with me? Leave me, Jacques. Why do
you want to marry me? Why take for yourself
what belongs to God? The hand of God is
on me and you can not defend me. Jacques,
we shall not be husband and wife in this
world.

JACQUES: What are these strange words, Violaine, so tender and bitter? What insidious
deadly paths are you leading me along? I think
you want to test me and mock me because
I am a simple farmer. You are beautiful, Violaine, and yet I am afraid of you when I see
you in this costume. It is not the dress of a

woman, but the clothing of the altar servant, of the one who helps the priest. It uncovers the flank and leaves the arms free. I can see that the spirit of Monsanvierge lives in you and you are the supreme flower outside of the enclosed garden. That face you are turning toward me is not of this world, it is not my Violaine. There are enough angels serving mass in heaven. Have pity on me who am a man without wings! I was happy with the companion God had given me, happy that I would hear her sigh with her head on my shoulders. Sweet bird! heaven is beautiful, but it is also a thing of wonder to be held as a woman. Heaven is beautiful, but so also is the heart of a man which is filled and no part is left empty, and it is worthy of God. Don't cause me to sin by leaving me. It is true, I am a man without knowledge and beauty, but I love you. You are my angel, my queen, my beloved!

VIOLAINE: So I have warned you to no purpose. You want to take me as a wife and you won't be turned away from this plan?

JACQUES: No, Violaine.

VIOLAINE: When a man takes a woman, they make only one soul and one flesh and nothing can separate them.

[228]

JACQUES: Yes, Violaine!

VIOLAINE: That is your will. It is not right then for me to hold anything back and to keep for myself any longer my great, unspeakable secret.

JACQUES: Again, Violaine, you speak of a secret.

VIOLAINE: Truly it is so great that your heart will be surfeited with it, that you will ask nothing more from me, and that we shall never again be separated. It is so profound a message that life, Jacques, and hell and heaven will not interrupt it, and they will never interrupt this moment when I revealed it to you in the blaze of this terrible sun here present which makes it hard for us to see one another's face.

JACQUES: Well, speak then!

VIOLAINE: First, tell me once again that you love me.

JACQUES: I love you.

VIOLAINE: And that I am your wife and your one love.

JACQUES: My wife, my one love.

VIOLAINE: Is it true, Jacques, that my face and my soul are not enough, and that you too have been deceived by my words? I want you to know the fire that is devouring me and my body that you have loved. Come closer. Closer! Still closer! Here against my side. Sit down on this bench. [*Silence.*] Give me your knife.

> [*He gives her his knife. She cuts into the linen cloth on her side, at the spot over her heart and under the left breast, and leaning toward him, she opens the cloth and shows him the flesh where the first sign of leprosy is apparent.*]

JACQUES [*turns aside*]: Give me my knife. [*She gives it back. Silence. Then Jacques walks off a few steps, half turning his back. He doesn't look at her through the rest of the act.*] Can I be mistaken? What is that silver flower emblazoned on your flesh?

VIOLAINE: You are not mistaken.

JACQUES: It's the disease, Violaine?

VIOLAINE: Yes, Jacques.

JACQUES: Leprosy?

VIOLAINE: You are hard to convince. You have to see to believe.

JACQUES: Which is the worse, leprosy of the soul or of the body?

VIOLAINE: I only know one. Leprosy of the body is a great enough evil.

JACQUES: So you don't know the other, wicked Violaine?

VIOLAINE: I am not wicked.

JACQUES: Infamous, wicked! Wicked in your soul and your flesh!

VIOLAINE: So, Jacques, you're not asking to marry me any more?

JACQUES: Stop blaspheming, child of the devil.

VIOLAINE: This is the great love you had for me.

JACQUES: This is the flower I had chosen.

VIOLAINE: This is the man who has taken my father's place.

JACQUES: This is the angel God sent me.

VIOLAINE: "Ah! who can separate us? I love you, Jacques, and you will defend me, and I know I have nothing to fear in your arms."

JACQUES: Stop saying those terrible words.

VIOLAINE: Didn't I keep my word? Wasn't my soul sufficient? Have you had enough of my body now? Are you going to forget Violaine and the heart she revealed to you?

JACQUES: Get away from me.

VIOLAINE: I'm far enough away. You have nothing to fear.

JACQUES: Yes, farther away than you were from your leper friend, whose flesh rottens on his skeleton.

VIOLAINE: Are you speaking of Pierre de Craon?

[231]

JACQUES: Yes. The man you kissed on the mouth.

VIOLAINE: Who told you that?

JACQUES: Mara saw you with her own eyes. She told me everything. It was her duty. But I didn't believe her. Confess it. Tell me now. It is true, isn't it?

VIOLAINE: It is true, Jacques. Mara always tells the truth.

JACQUES: It's true that you kissed him?

VIOLAINE: It is true.

JACQUES: You're wicked. Are you so fond of the flames of hell that you coveted them alive?

VIOLAINE [*low*]: Not wicked. Sweet Violaine.

JACQUES: Do you deny that man had you and possessed you?

VIOLAINE: I deny nothing, Jacques.

JACQUES: But I still love you, Violaine! I beg you, if there's something you can say, I'll believe it. Just tell me it isn't true.

VIOLAINE: I can't turn black in one moment, but in just a few months you won't recognize me.

JACQUES: Tell me that it isn't true.

VIOLAINE: Mara always tells the truth and you saw the flower on my flesh.

[232]

JACQUES: Farewell, Violaine!

VIOLAINE: Farewell, Jacques!

JACQUES: What are you going to do now?

VIOLAINE: Take off these clothes. Leave the house. Fulfill the law. Show myself to the priest. Then find . . .

JACQUES: Go on.

VIOLAINE: . . . the place reserved for people like me. The lepers' colony of Géyn.

JACQUES: When are you doing all that?

VIOLAINE: Today. This very evening. [*Silence.*] There is nothing else to do.

JACQUES: We must avoid a scandal. Take off these clothes and put on a dress for travelling. I will tell you the right thing to do.

[*They leave.*]

SCENE IV

[*Room of the first act.*]

MOTHER: The fine weather is still with us. Eight days now without rain. From time to time we can hear the bells of Arcy. Ding! dong! How warm it is! How huge everything is! What is Violaine doing? and Jacques? Why are they taking so long for their talk? I am

[233]

sorry I said that to her. [*She sighs.*] What is my old husband doing? Where is he now? Ah! [*She bends her head.*]

MARA [*entering abruptly*]: They're coming here. I think the marriage is broken off. Do you hear? Don't open your mouth.

MOTHER: You're a sly wicked girl. You've gotten what you wanted.

MARA: Say nothing. The bad moment will be over soon. It wouldn't have taken place anyway since it's me he should marry and not her. It will be better for her that way. This is the way it had to be. Do you hear? Don't talk.

MOTHER: Who told you that story?

MARA: I don't need to be told things. Every thing was written on their faces. I caught them in the act. In a flash I knew the truth. And I pitied Jacques, the poor fellow.

MOTHER: I am sorry about what I said.

MARA: You said nothing, you know nothing, you must say nothing! And if they say anything to you, no matter what they tell you, repeat their words and do as they want. Nothing else can be done.

SCENE V

[*Enter Jacques Hury, then Violaine in black, dressed as for travelling.*]

MOTHER: What has happened, Jacques? Why are you dressed that way, Violaine, as if you were going to leave?

VIOLAINE: I too am going to leave.

MOTHER: What has happened between you that you also are going to leave?

JACQUES: Nothing has happened. You know that I went to see my mother in Braine and that I've just returned from there.

MOTHER: Yes, I know that.

JACQUES: You know that she is old and crippled. Well, she said that before she dies, she wants to see her daughter-in-law and give her her blessing.

MOTHER: Can't she wait for the wedding?

JACQUES: She is sick, she can't wait. And this season for the harvest, when there is so much work to be done, isn't the right time for the wedding. Violaine and I have just been talking it over, and we decided it is better to wait for the fall. Meanwhile she will stay with my mother in Braine.

MOTHER: Is that what you want, Violaine?

VIOLAINE: Yes, mother.

MOTHER: But do you have to leave today?

VIOLAINE: Yes, this very evening.

JACQUES: I will go with her. I haven't much time because of the haying and havesting this month. Already I've been away too long.

MOTHER: Stay, Violaine! I don't want you to go away too.

VIOLAINE: It's only for a short time, mother.

MOTHER: Do you promise that, just for a short time?

JACQUES: Just a short time, and when the fall comes, she'll be back again with us and never leave us.

MOTHER: Jacques, why are you letting her go?

JACQUES: Don't you think it is hard for me too?

MARA: What they are saying makes good sense, mother.

MOTHER: I hate to see my child leave me.

VIOLAINE: Don't be sad. What difference will just a few days make? We have to let just a little time go by. I know how much you love me. And Mara too, and Jacques my fiancé. He and I belong to one another and nothing can separate us. Look at me, Jacques. He is crying because I am leaving. This isn't the time to

[236]

cry, mother. I'm young and beautiful, and everyone loves me. I know, my father went away, but he left me with a kind husband, a friend who will never desert me. You see, this isn't the time to cry but to rejoice. How beautiful life is and how happy I am!

MARA: What do you say, Jacques? You don't seem very glad.

JACQUES: Isn't it natural that I should be sad?

MARA: But it's only a separation of a few months.

JACQUES: That's too long for my heart.

MARA: Did you hear how nicely he said that, Violaine? But you too are sad. Try to smile with that charming mouth of yours. Raise those blue eyes our father loved so much. Jacques, look at your wife and see how beautiful she is when she smiles. No one will take her from you. What man could be sad when he has such a beauty to adorn his house? See that you love her well. Tell her to be full of courage.

JACQUES: Take courage, Violaine. You haven't lost me. We haven't lost one another. If I don't doubt your love, must you doubt mine? I love you, Violaine, and I am sure of your love. My mother knows about you and will be happy to see you. It is hard to leave the house of your parents. But where you are going, you will be well taken care of. Your love and your innocence will not be harmed.

MOTHER: These are kind words, but there is something strange about them, something I don't like, and it's the same with what you have said, my child.

MARA: I don't see anything strange, mother.

MOTHER: If I hurt you a little while ago, Violaine, forget what I said.

VIOLAINE: You didn't hurt me.

MOTHER: Let me embrace you then.

[*She opens her arms.*]

VIOLAINE: No, mother.

MOTHER: What do you mean?

VIOLAINE: No.

MARA: This is wrong, Violaine. Can't we touch you now? Why do you treat us like lepers?

VIOLAINE: I have taken a vow.

MARA: What vow?

VIOLAINE: That no one will touch me.

MARA: Do you mean, until you return?

[*Silence. Violaine lowers her head.*]

JACQUES: Leave her alone. Can't you see how upset she is?

[238]

MOTHER: Leave us alone for a minute. [*They go off.*] You can't lie to me, child, you won't lie to your own mother. What I said was hard for me to say, but I'm an old woman who is full of sorrow. You are young and you will forget. My husband has gone and now you are leaving me. My own suffering is nothing and the suffering I give to others makes me unable to eat. Don't forget that, my lamb. You can be proud that you've hurt no one. I gave you the best advice I could. Don't blame me, Violaine. Save your sister. She mustn't ruin herself. God is with you and that is your reward. You may never see my face again. The Lord be with you. If you don't want to kiss me, at least I can give you my blessing, sweet Violaine.

VIOLAINE: Yes, mother!

> [*She kneels and the mother makes the sign of the cross over her.*]

JACQUES [*returning*]: Come, Violaine, it is time to go.

MARA: Pray for us.

VIOLAINE [*calling out*]: Take all my dresses, Mara, all my things! And don't be afraid. I didn't touch them. I didn't go into that room.

[239]

Take my wedding-dress, it's so pretty!
> [*She stretches out her arm as if seeking a support. All stand off from her. She leaves with uncertain steps, followed by Jacques.*]

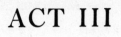

ACT III

SCENE I

Chevoche. A large forest with sparse trees, made up principally of very high oaks and birches, and below them, pine trees, fir trees and some holly. A wide opening has recently been made in the wood to the horizon. Workmen are taking away tree-trunks and preparing the highway. Encampment on the side, with huts of fagots, fire and kettle, etc. It is in a sand-pit where a few workmen are loading fine white sand on to a small cart. An apprentice of Pierre de Craon is in charge. He is crouching on a pile of dry broom. On both sides of the new road you see colossi made of fagots, with a collar and old coat of white cloth, and a red cross on the chest, a cask for the head whose edges are cut like the teeth of a saw as if to make a crown, with a face grossly painted in red. A long trumpet is fixed in the bunghole and supported by a board as if it were an arm. Twilight. Snow on the ground and overcast sky. Xmas eve.

MAYOR OF CHEVOCHE: Now the king can come.
WORKER: He can come now. The work's done.
MAYOR [*with satisfaction*]: It's a fine job. And everyone helped out, all that could, men, women and children. And this was the worst part, with all the filth of briars and swamp.

The lads of Bruyères weren't able to outdo us.

WORKER: Their road is still cluttered with all the stumps they've left.

[*Laughter.*]

APPRENTICE [*pedantically, with a sharp piercing voice*]: Vox clamantis in deserto: Parate vias Domini et erunt prava in directa et aspera in vias planas. Yes, you've done good work! And I congratulate you. It's a path for Corpus Christi. [*Pointing out the giants.*] Gentlemen. who are these fine respectable people?

WORKER: Handsome, aren't they? The old drunk Père Vincent made them. He says it's the great king of Abyssinia and his wife Bellotte.

APPRENTICE: I thought they were Gog and Magog.

MAYOR: They're the two angels of Chevoche here to greet their king. We'll set fire to them when he's gone. Listen.

[*All listen.*]

WORKER: It isn't him yet. We'd hear the bells of Bruyères.

OTHER WORKER: He won't come before midnight. He ate supper at Fisme.

[244]

ANOTHER: This is a good place to see from. I'm not budging.

ANOTHER: Have ya anything to eat, Perrot? All I have is a frozen piece of bread.

MAYOR: Don't be worried. There's a gammon of pork in the kettle and sausages and the roe-buck we killed; and three ells of sausage and potatoes and a good cask of Marne wine.

APPRENTICE: I'm staying with you.

A WOMAN: It's a good little Christmas.

APPRENTICE: It was on Christmas day that King Clovis was baptized in Reims.

OTHER WOMAN: It's on Christmas day our King Charles is coming back to be consecrated.

ANOTHER: He's being brought back here by a simple girl, sent by God.

ANOTHER: She's called Jeanne.

ANOTHER: The maid!

ANOTHER: Who was born on Twelfth Night.

ANOTHER: Who chased the English out of Or-léans which they were besieging.

ANOTHER: And who is going to chase them all out of France. So be it!

WORKER [*humming*]: Noël! Ki ki ki. Noël! Brr. It's freezing!

[*He pulls his cloak around him.*]

WOMAN: You have to look hard to find a little fellow dressed in red who is near the king. It's her.

ANOTHER: On a big black horse.

THE FIRST: Only six months ago she guarded the flocks of her father.

ANOTHER: And now she holds a banner with the name of Jesus on it.

WORKER: The English run from it like mice.

ANOTHER: Look out for the bad Burgundians of Saponay.

ANOTHER: They'll all be in Reims by early morning.

ANOTHER: What's going to happen in Reims?

APPRENTICE: The two bells of the cathedral, Baudon and Baude, will begin to ring at the "Gloria" of midnight mass, and they won't stop ringing until the French come. Everyone will keep a candle lighted at home until morning. They'll wait until the king comes for the mass at dawn, the "Lux fulgebit." All the priests will go to meet him, three hundred priests with the archbishop in golden copes, and the regular priests, and the mayor and the townspeople. It will be a sight to see on the snow under the clear lively sun and all the people singing Noël. They say the king plans

[246]

to get down from his horse and enter the city on an ass, like Our Lord.

MAYOR: Why didn't you stay there?

APPRENTICE: Maître Pierre de Craon sent me to get sand.

MAYOR: Is that what he's working at now?

APPRENTICE: He says there isn't much time.

MAYOR: Is there a better way to spend it than on making this road, like the rest of us?

APPRENTICE: He says his work is not to make roads for the king, but a dwelling for God.

MAYOR: What's the use of Reims, if the king can't get there?

APPRENTICE: What's the use of the road, if there's no church at the end?

MAYOR: He isn't much of a Frenchman.

APPRENTICE: He claims to know only his trade. The man who talks politics in France gets his nose blackened with the bottom of the frying-pan.

MAYOR: He's been ten years trying to finish his cathedral of Justitia.

APPRENTICE: That's right! The stone work is finished and the frame is in position. All that remains is the steeple which is still growing.

MAYOR: They're not working very hard at it now.

APPRENTICE: The master is preparing to make the windows and that's why he sent us here to get sand. It isn't his profession and yet all winter he worked at the furnaces. It's harder to make light than to make gold. To blow on that heavy matter and make it transparent "as our bodies of clay will be changed into glorified bodies," says Saint Paul. For every color he says he wants to find the mother color, as it was made by God. That is why he pours into large pure vases filled with clear water hyacinth, ultramarine, soft gold, vermillion, and looks at the handsome rose windows from the inside and the effect they have in the sun and the grace of God, and how they turn and bloom in the matrass. He says there is not one color he can't make just with his mind, as his body makes red and blue. He wants Justitia of Reims on her wedding day to shine like dawn itself.

MAYOR: People say he's a leper.

APPRENTICE: That's not true! I saw him naked last summer when he was swimming in the Aisne at Soissons. I can swear it. His flesh was as healthy as a child's.

MAYOR: There's something queer about him. Why did he stay in hiding for so long?

[248]

APPRENTICE: That's a lie!

MAYOR: But I know, I'm older than you. Don't lose your temper, my boy. There's nothing wrong in having a sickness in one's body. He doesn't work inside his body.

APPRENTICE: He better not hear you say that! I remember how he punished one of us who stayed all the time in a corner drawing. He sent him for the whole day on the scaffolding with the masons to help them and pass them their mortar-troughs and their stones, saying that at the end of the day he'd know two things better than by rules and drawing: the weight a man can carry and the height of his body. And just as the grace of God multiplies each of our good actions, that is how he taught us what he calls the "shekel of the Temple," and that house of God of which each man who does what he can with his body is like a secret foundation. He taught us what the thumb is and the hand and the cubit and our span and the extended arm and the circle you make with it, and the foot and the step, and how nothing of all that is ever the same. Do you think the body was of no consequence to Noah when he made the ark? Everything is important: the number of steps between the door and the

[249]

altar, the height to which the eyes can reach, the number of souls that can be contained in the two side aisles of the church. The Pagan artist did everything with the outside, and we do everything with the inside like bees, as the soul does for the body. Nothing is inert. Everything lives, everything is an act of thanksgiving.

MAYOR: Listen to the little man speak.

WORKER: He's like a magpie full of the words of his master.

APPRENTICE: Speak respectfully of Pierre de Craon.

MAYOR: He is indeed a bourgeois of Reims and he's called the master of the compass, as they used to call Messire Loys the master of the ruler.

ANOTHER: Throw some wood into the fire, Perrot, it's beginning to snow.

[*Night has come. Enter Mara in black, carrying a kind of package under her cloak.*]

MARA: Are you from Chevoche?

MAYOR: We are.

MARA: Praised be Jesus Christ!

MAYOR: Amen!

MARA: Is the place of Géyn in your town?

MAYOR: Where the leper lives?

MARA: Yes.

MAYOR: Not exactly in the town, but close by.

ANOTHER: Do you want to see her?

MARA: Yes.

MAN: You can't see her. She always keeps a veil over her face, according to the law.

ANOTHER: It's a good law. I for one don't want to see her.

MARA: Has she been with you for a long time?

MAN: A little more than six years and we wish she was out of the way.

MARA: Does she do any harm?

MAN: No, but it's bad luck all the same to have vermine like her around.

MAYOR: And the township has to feed her.

MAN: I've just remembered. We forgot to take her food to her three days now because of this work on the road.

WOMAN: What do you want with that woman?
            [*Mara doesn't answer and remains standing, looking into the fire.*]

WOMAN: What you're holding in your arms looks as if it might be a baby.

ANOTHER: It's too cold to carry small children around at this hour.

MARA: It's not cold.

[251]

[*Silence. In the night under the trees can be heard the noise of a wooden rattle.*]

OLD WOMAN: There she is. That's the sound she makes. Mother of God, what a pity she isn't dead!

WOMAN: She's come for her food. No fear she'll forget.

MAN: It's a chore to have to feed such vermine.

ANOTHER: Throw her something. Don't let her come any closer. She could give us the disease.

ANOTHER: No meat, Perrot! It's a fast day, Christmas eve! [*They laugh.*] Throw her this loaf of bread that's all frozen. It's good enough for her.

MAN [*shouting*]: Hey, you, without a face! hey! Jeanne-who's-eaten-away! [*The black form of the leper can be seen against the snow. Mara looks at her.*] Catch!

>[*He throws her a piece of bread. She bends down and picks it up, then moves off. Mara starts walking after her.*]

MAN: Where's she going?

ANOTHER: Hey, you, wher'ya going? What are you doing?

>[*They move off.*]

SCENE II

They go through a forest, leave tracks in the snow. Come to a clearing. The moon with a huge halo lights up a mound covered with heather and white sand. Monstrous stones, sandstone in fantastic forms. They resemble prehistoric animals, inexplicable monuments, idols with ill-formed heads and arms. The leper leads Mara to the cave where she lives, a kind of low corridor where she can't stand up. The back is closed save for an opening for smoke.

SCENE III

VIOLAINE: Who are you, who aren't afraid to follow after a leper? To be close to me is dangerous. My breath is harmful.

MARA: It's me, Violaine.

VIOLAINE: It's so long since I heard that voice. Is it you, mother?

MARA: It's me, Violaine.

VIOLAINE: It's your voice and another's. Let me light this fire. It's very cold. And this torch also.

[*She lights a fire of peat and heather,*

from embers kept in a pot; then the torch.]

MARA: It's me, Violaine. Mara, your sister.

VIOLAINE: Dear sister, how good you are to come! But aren't you afraid to be here?

MARA: I'm afraid of nothing.

VIOLAINE: Your voice is like our mother's.

MARA: Our mother is dead.

[*Silence.*]

VIOLAINE: When did she die?

MARA: The very month after you left.

VIOLAINE: Did she know about me?

MARA: I am not sure.

VIOLAINE: Poor Mama! May God love her!

MARA: Our father hasn't yet come back.

VIOLAINE: How about you and Jacques?

MARA: All is fine.

VIOLAINE: All is as you want it at home?

MARA: All is fine.

VIOLAINE: I knew it would be that way with you and Jacques.

MARA: You should see what we've done. We have three new ploughs. You wouldn't recognize Combernon. And we are going to take down the old walls, now that the king has come back.

VIOLAINE: Are you happy together, Mara?

[254]

MARA: Yes, we are happy. We love one another.

VIOLAINE: Thanks be to God!

MARA: Violaine! Can you see what I have in my arms?

VIOLAINE: I can't see.

MARA: Lift up your veil.

VIOLAINE: There's another under this one.

MARA: Can't you see at all?

VIOLAINE: I have no eyes. Only my soul is alive in this diseased body.

MARA: You're blind? How do you make your way so well?

VIOLAINE: I hear.

MARA: What do you mean?

VIOLAINE: I hear things existing around me.

MARA [*solemnly*]: Can you hear me, Violaine?

VIOLAINE: God gave me understanding which He has given to everyone.

MARA: Do you hear me, Violaine?

VIOLAINE: Poor Mara!

MARA: Do you hear me?

VIOLAINE: What do you want from me, dear sister?

MARA: I want to praise with you the God who gave you leprosy.

VIOLAINE: We shall praise Him on the eve of His Birth.

MARA: It is easy to be a saint when leprosy serves you.

VIOLAINE: I know nothing about that, since I am not a saint.

MARA: One has to turn to God when there is nothing else left.

VIOLAINE: At least He will not fail us.

MARA [*sweetly*]: Perhaps, but who can tell, Violaine?

VIOLAINE: There is no life but only death where I am.

MARA: Heretic! are you certain of your salvation?

VIOLAINE: I am certain of His goodness which has cared for me.

MARA: We can see an earnest of that.

VIOLAINE: I believe in God who gave me my share of the world.

MARA: What can you know about an invisible God who appears nowhere?

VIOLAINE: For me He is no more invisible than the world is.

MARA [*ironically*]: So, He's with you, little dove, and He loves you?

VIOLAINE: Yes, He's with all those who suffer.

MARA: I know, His love is boundless.

[256]

VIOLAINE: It is like the love of fire for wood when it catches on.

MARA: He has punished you hard.

VIOLAINE: Not more than I deserved.

MARA: And the man you gave yourself to has already forgotten you.

VIOLAINE: I never gave myself to a man.

MARA: Sweet lying Violaine! Didn't I see you tenderly embrace Pierre de Craon on a beautiful June morning?

VIOLAINE: You saw everything. There was nothing else to see.

MARA: Why did you kiss him as if he were so precious?

VIOLAINE: The poor man was a leper and I was full of happiness that day.

MARA: And so you did it in all innocence?

VIOLAINE: Like a little girl who kisses a poor small boy.

MARA: Can I believe you, Violaine?

VIOLAINE: It is true.

MARA: Don't tell me it was willingly you left me Jacques.

VIOLAINE: No, not willingly. I loved him. I am not so perfect.

MARA: Did you expect him to love you still when you were a leper?

VIOLAINE: No, I didn't expect it.

MARA: Who could ever love a leper?

VIOLAINE: My heart is pure.

MARA: But how could Jacques know this? He looks upon you as a criminal.

VIOLAINE: Our mother had told me that you loved him.

MARA: Don't tell me that she made you a leper.

VIOLAINE: God cautioned me with His grace.

MARA: So that when our mother spoke to you . . .

VIOLAINE: . . . It was still His voice I heard.

MARA: But why let people think you perjured yourself?

VIOLAINE: Wasn't it up to me to do something? Poor Jacques! Was it right to leave him sorrowing for me?

MARA: Say that you didn't love him.

VIOLAINE: That I didn't love him, Mara?

MARA: Well, I couldn't have let him go.

VIOLAINE: Did I let him go?

MARA: I would have died.

VIOLAINE: Am I living?

MARA: Now I'm happy with him.

VIOLAINE: God bless both of you!

MARA: I gave him a child, Violaine. A dear little girl. A sweet baby.

[258]

VIOLAINE: God bless you!

MARA: We have known great joy. But yours is greater with God.

VIOLAINE: I too knew that joy eight years ago and my heart was filled with it, so full that I foolishly asked God that it last and never be over. And God in His strange way listened to me. I will never be cured of my leprosy as long as there remains a part of my flesh to be devoured. The love in my heart will never be cured as long as there is an immortal soul in me to nourish it. Does your husband know you, Mara?

MARA: Does any man know a woman?

VIOLAINE: Happy is the woman who can really be known and give herself completely. What would Jacques have done with all I could have given him?

MARA: You transferred your faith to Another.

VIOLAINE: Love creates grief and grief creates Love. The wood you set fire to gives ashes and a flame also.

MARA: What is the use of a blind piece of wood which gives neither light nor warmth to others?

VIOLAINE: Isn't it enough that it serve me? Don't begrudge that light to the calcinated creature whose very depths are burned, and who shows the fire within herself. If you spent one single night in my body, you wouldn't say that this fire has no warmth. The male is a priest, but it is not forbidden a woman to be the victim. God is avaricious and doesn't allow any creature to be kindled without some impurity being consumed, her own and that around her, like the embers of the censer which are stirred. Today's suffering is everywhere. The people have no father. They look about them and find no king and no pope. That is why my body is suffering in the place of Christendom as it disintegrates. Suffering is powerful when it is willed as sin is. So, you saw me kiss the leper, Mara? The cup of sorrow is deep. Whoever puts his lips to it once does not remove them easily.

MARA: Then take my suffering with yours!

VIOLAINE: I have already taken it.

MARA: Violaine, if some part of you is still alive, which is my sister under that veil and within your useless body, remember that we were children together. Have pity on me!

VIOLAINE: What is on your mind, dear sister? You can tell me.

MARA: I am brokenhearted. My grief is greater than yours.

[260]

VIOLAINE: Is it greater?

[*Mara, with a cry opens her cloak and holds out in her arms the corpse of a baby.*]

MARA: Look! Take it!

VIOLAINE: What is it?

MARA: Look! Take it! Here it is!

[*She puts the corpse in Violaine's arms.*]

VIOLAINE: Ah! its little body is stiff. Its poor little face is cold.

MARA: Violaine, it's my child. A little girl. Her face was sweet. This is her poor body.

VIOLAINE [*low voice*]: Is she dead, Mara?

MARA: You take her. You can have her.

VIOLAINE: May you be comforted, Mara!

MARA: They wanted to take her away from me, but I wouldn't let them. I left the house and kept her in my arms. You take her now, Violaine. I'm giving her to you.

VIOLAINE: What can I do, Mara?

MARA: What can you do? Don't you understand? I tell you she's dead. She's dead.

VIOLAINE: Her soul is with God. She is following the Lamb. She is with all the other blessed children.

MARA: But for me she is dead.

[261]

VIOLAINE: You're giving me her body. Give the rest to God.

MARA: No, I won't be tricked with your words of a nun. No, I won't be consoled. The milk which burns in my breast cries to God like the blood of Abel. Are there fifty children to be taken from my body? fifty souls to be taken from my soul? Do you know what it is to be torn in two and give birth to a tiny being that cries? The mid-wife told me I would have no more children. But no matter how many I had, it wouldn't be Aubaine.

VIOLAINE: You must accept this.

MARA: You know how stubborn I am. I cannot be resigned. I accept nothing.

VIOLAINE: Poor sister!

MARA: Her cruel little mouth used to hurt me when it bit me inside.

VIOLAINE [*caressing its face*]: How cold her face is!

MARA: He doesn't know yet.

VIOLAINE: He wasn't at home, then?

MARA: He was in Reims, selling the wheat. She died suddenly, in two hours.

VIOLAINE: Whom did she look like?

MARA: Like him, Violaine. She's not only mine, she is his too. Only her eyes are mine.

VIOLAINE: Poor Jacques!

MARA: I didn't come here just to have you say, poor Jacques!

VIOLAINE: What do you want of me?

MARA: Violaine, do you know what it means to damn one's soul? Deliberately, for all time? Do you know what is in your heart when you really blaspheme? When I was running, there was a devil singing me a song. Do you want to know what he taught me?

VIOLAINE: Don't speak such terrible things.

MARA: Give me back my child I gave you.

VIOLAINE: It was dead when you gave it.

MARA: Give it back to me alive.

VIOLAINE: What are you saying, Mara?

MARA: I will not accept the death of my child.

VIOLAINE: Is it in my power to bring back the dead?

MARA: I don't know, but you're the only one I can come to.

VIOLAINE: Only God can resurrect the dead.

MARA: What good are you then?

VIOLAINE: For suffering and praying.

MARA: What is the good of suffering and praying if you don't give me back my child?

VIOLAINE: God can answer that. It is enough that I serve Him.

MARA: I'm deaf. I can't hear. I'm calling to you from far off, Violaine. Give me back that child I gave you. I'm bending before you. Have pity on me! Give me back that child you took from me.

VIOLAINE: The One who took her can give her back.

MARA: Give her back to me, then. I know it's all your fault.

VIOLAINE: My fault, Mara?

MARA: It's mine then. But give her back to me, sister.

VIOLAINE: You can see that she's dead.

MARA: You lie! She isn't dead. You're weak and silly. If I could get close to God as you can, He wouldn't snatch my children away from me that easily.

VIOLAINE: Ask me to create the world all over again!

MARA: But it is written that you can blow on a mountain and cast it into the sea.

VIOLAINE: I could if I were a saint.

MARA: You have to be a saint when a poor woman begs you.

VIOLAINE: That is the greatest of the temptations. I swear before God that I am not a saint.

MARA: Give me back my child.

[264]

VIOLAINE: Lord, You see into my heart. I swear before God I am not a saint.

MARA: Give me back my child.

VIOLAINE: Why don't you leave me in peace? Why come to torment me in my grave? I am worth nothing. I can't do God's work, I am not like God. You are asking me to judge the work of God.

MARA: I am only asking you for my child.

[*Pause.*]

VIOLAINE [*raising her finger*]: Listen.

[*Silence. Bells at a distance, imperceptible.*]

MARA: I hear nothing.

VIOLAINE: The Christmas bells, announcing midnight mass. A child is born to us, Mara!

MARA: Give me back mine.

[*Trumpets far off.*]

VIOLAINE: What is that?

MARA: The king going to Reims. Didn't you hear about the road the peasants are cutting through the forest? That will give them plenty of wood. He's being led by a shepherd, through the center of France, to Reims where he'll be consecrated.

VIOLAINE: Praise be to God for accomplishing such things!

[265]

[*Bell, again, clear.*]

MARA: The bells are ringing the "Gloria." The wind is carrying the sound to us. Three villages are ringing bells at the same time.

VIOLAINE: Let us pray with the universe. Are you cold, Mara?

MARA: Only my heart is cold.

VIOLAINE: Pray with me. We haven't been together at Christmas for so long. Do not be afraid. I have taken your suffering as mine. Look! What you gave me is hidden against my heart. Stop crying. This is no time to cry when the hope of all men has just been born.

[*Bell, far off, less distinct.*]

MARA: It's stopped snowing and the stars are out.

VIOLAINE: Do you see this book? The priest who comes to visit me from time to time left it here.

MARA: I see it.

VIOLAINE: Won't you take it and read me the Christmas office, the first lesson of each of the Three Nocturnes.

MARA [*takes the book and reads*]:

The Prophecy of Isaias:

"Land of Zabulon and Nephthali, its burden at first how lightly borne! but afterwards affliction weighed on it, Galilee, by the sea road

[266]

where the Gentiles dwell west of Jordan. And now the people that went about in darkness has seen a great light; for men abiding in a land where death overshadowed them, light has dawned. Their number thou didst increase, but gavest them no joy of it; now, they shall rejoice when the harvest is in, as men triumph when victory is won, and booty taken, and they fall to dividing up the spoils. Yoke that fixed the burden, shaft that galled the shoulder, rod of the tyrant, all lie broken now, as they did long ago, when Madian fell. All the trophies of the old tumultuous forays, all the panoply stained with blood, will be burnt up now, will go to feed the flames. For our sakes a child is born, to our race a son is given, whose shoulder will bear the sceptre of princely power. What name shall be given him? Peerless among counsellors, the mighty God, Father of the world to come, the Prince of peace."

VIOLAINE [*looking up*]: Listen!

       [*Silence.*]

VOICES OF ANGELS:

    [*in the sky, heard only by Violaine.*]

CHORUS: Hodie nobis de caelo pax vera descendit, hodie per totum mundum melliflui facti sunt caeli.

SINGLE VOICE: Hodie illuxit nobis dies redemptionis novae, redemptionis novae, reparationis antiquae, felicitatis aeternae.

CHOIR: Hodie per totum mundum melliflui facti sunt caeli.

> [*Violaine raises her finger. Silence. Mara listens and seems worried.*]

MARA: I hear nothing.

VIOLAINE: Go on with the reading, Mara.

MARA [*continuing*]:

> *Sermon of Saint Leo, Pope*

"Beloved, our Saviour was born on this day. Let us rejoice. There is no opening unto sadness when it is the birthday of life. The consumed fear of death gives us the joy of promised eternity. No one is excluded from this joy. The same reason for happiness is common to all, since Our Lord, destroyer of sin and death, since He found no one exempt from fault, came to free all. Let the saint rejoice, for his palm is near at hand. Let the sinner rejoice . . ."

> [*Prolonged blast from trumpets, quite close. Shouts in the forest.*]

VOICES: The king! The king! The king of France!

[*Two more trumpet flourishes, ear-splitting, solemn, triumphant.*]

MARA: The king of France is on his way to Reims. [*Silence.*] Violaine! [*Silence.*] Do you hear me, Violaine? [*Silence. She resumes the reading.*] ". . . Let the sinner rejoice because he is invited to forgiveness! Let the Gentile hope because he is invited to life! For the Son of God according to the fullness of that time which the inscrutability of Divine Counsel arranged, to reconcile it with its maker, was clothed in the nature of man, so that the inventor of death, Satan, would be in his turn subjugated by the death he had conquered."

VOICES OF ANGELS:

[*heard only by Violaine, as before.*]

CHOIR: O magnum mysterium et admirabile sacramentum ut animalia viderent Dominum natum jacentem in praesepio! Beata Virgo cujus viscera meruerunt portare Dominum Christum.

SINGLE VOICE: Ave Maria, gratia plena, Dominus tecum.

CHOIR: Beata Virgo cujus viscera meruerunt portare Dominum Christum.

MARA: I am not worthy to read this book, Violaine. I know I am too hard. I am sorry for this. I wish I could be different.

VIOLAINE: Go on reading, Mara. You don't realize who is singing the response.

[*Silence.*]

MARA [*with an effort, takes up the book, and in a trembling voice*]:

The Holy Gospel according to Saint Luke.

[*They both stand up.*]

"It happened that a decree went out at this time from the emperor Augustus, enjoining that the whole world should be registered."

[*They sit down.*]

Homily of Saint Gregory, Pope

[*She stops, overcome by emotion. The trumpets sound for the last time in the distance.*]

"Because, through the grace of God, we are to celebrate today the holy mass three times, we cannot speak for any length of the gospel which has just been read. Yet the birth of our Redeemer obliges me to say to you at least a few words. Why was a census of the world taken at the time of this birth, unless it was to show that he who appeared in the flesh would take the census of his saints for eternity? Yet the prophet says of the wicked: they will be

[270]

stricken from the book of the living and they
will not be written down among the just. It
was a good thing that Bethlehem was the place
of his birth. Bethlehem means "house of bread"
and Jesus Christ said of himself: "I am the
living bread from heaven." The place there-
fore where Our Lord was born had first been
called the house of bread, so that he appeared
in the form of flesh who was to feed our hearts
on spiritual food. He was born, not in the
house of his parents, but on the roadside,
doubtless to show that, in the humanity with
which he was clothed, he had been born in a
foreign place."

VOICES OF ANGELS:

CHOIR: Beata viscera Mariae Virginis quae por-
taverunt aeterni Patris Filium; et beata ubera
quae lactaverunt Christum Dominum. Qui
hodie pro salute mundi de Virgine nasci dignatus est.

SINGLE VOICE: Dies sanctificatus illuxit nobis,
venite, gentes, et adorate Dominum.

CHOIR: Qui hodie pro salute mundi de Virgine
nasci dignatus est.

[*Long silence.*]

VOICES OF ANGELS: [*again, almost imperceptible*]:

CHOIR: Verbum caro factum est et habitavit in nobis; et vidimus gloriam ejus, gloriam quasi Unigeniti a Patre, plenum gratiae et veritatis.

SINGLE VOICE: Omnia per ipsum facta sunt et sine ipso factum est nihil.

CHOIR: Et vidimus gloriam ejus, gloriam quasi Unigeniti a Patre, plenum gratiae et veritatis.

SINGLE VOICE: Gloria Patri et Filio et Spiritui Sancto.

CHOIR: Et vidimus gloriam ejus, gloriam quasi Unigeniti a Patre, plenum gratiae et veritatis. [*Long silence.*]

VIOLAINE [*suddenly utters a stifled cry*]: Ah!

MARA: What is it? [*With her hand she makes a sign to Mara to be silent. First streak of daylight. Violaine puts her hand under her cloak as if she were arranging her clothes.*] Violaine, something is moving under your cloak.

VIOLAINE [*as if gradually awakening*]: Is it you, Mara? Good morning, sister. I feel the breath of the new day on my face.

MARA: Violaine, are you moving your arm? What is under your cloak?

VIOLAINE: Peace, Mara! It is Christmas when joy is born.

MARA: What joy can there be for me unless my child lives.

VIOLAINE: A small child is born to us too.

MARA: In God's name what are you saying?

VIOLAINE: "Behold I bring you tidings of great joy . . ."

MARA: Something is moving under your cloak. [*The bare foot of a small child appears in the opening of the cloak, and moves lazily.*]

VIOLAINE: "Because a man came into the world." [*Mara falls on her knees, sighs deeply, her head on the knees of her sister. Violaine caresses her face.*] Poor sister! You're crying. You have suffered so much. [*Silence. She kisses her head.*] Take her, Mara. Are you going to leave the child with me forever?

MARA [*takes the child from under the cloak and looks at it passionately.*] It's alive!

VIOLAINE [*takes a few steps on the heather. Under the first rays of an icy dawn can be seen, first, trees, pines and birches, covered with frost, and then, at the end of a huge field, covered with snow, very small, at the top of a hill and clearly outlined in the pure air the silhouette of the five towers of Monsanvierge.*]: Praise be to God!

[273]

MARA: She is alive!

VIOLAINE: Peace on earth to men!

MARA: She is alive!

VIOLAINE: She is alive and we are. And the Father's face is over the new earth.

MARA: My child lives.

VIOLAINE [*raising her finger*]: Listen. [*Silence.*] I hear the angelus from Monsanvierge.

> [*She crosses herself and prays. The child awakens.*]

MARA [low voice]: It's me, Aubaine! Do you know me? [*The child moves and moans.*] There! my little darling! My treasure! [*The child opens her eyes, looks at her mother and begins to cry. Mara looks at her attentively.*] Violaine! What is the meaning of this? She had black eyes and now they are blue like yours. [*Silence.*] And what is that drop of milk I see on her lips?

ACT IV

SCENE I

The second part of the night. Room of the first act. In the fireplace the coals cast a feeble light. In the middle a long table with a narrow cloth which falls evenly on both sides. The double door is open—revealing a starry night. A lighted torch is placed in the middle of the table.

Enter Jacques Hury as if he were looking for someone. He goes out and brings back Mara by the arm.

JACQUES: What were you doing out there?

MARA: I thought I heard the noise of a cart way down in the valley.

JACQUES [*listening*]: I can't hear anything.

MARA: You never hear anything. I keep my eyes and ears open.

JACQUES: You'd do better to sleep.

MARA: You haven't been sleeping so well yourself.

JACQUES: I've been thinking, trying to understand.

MARA: What are you trying to understand?

JACQUES: Aubaine. She was sick and on the point of dying. And then one day I come home and they tell me that you had rushed off with her like a mad woman. That was Christmas. On the day of the Holy Innocents you return with the child. And she's cured.

MARA: It was a miracle.

JACQUES: Yes, sometimes you say it was the Virgin and other times you speak of some holy soul somewhere who performed the miracle.

MARA: It was neither one. I performed the miracle. Listen!

[*Startled, they listen.*]

JACQUES: I don't hear anything.

MARA [*trembling*]: Close that door. It bothers me.

[*He pushes the door.*]

JACQUES: What is certain is that her face is not the same. Oh! it's the same, but it isn't. Her eyes, for example, have changed.

MARA: Clever boy! Did you notice that all by yourself? That's what happens when the good Lord takes charge of our affairs. You take care of your own. [*Violently.*] Why do you keep looking at that door?

JACQUES: It's you who don't stop listening.

MARA: I'm waiting.

JACQUES: What are you waiting for? Who?

MARA: I'm waiting for my father, Anne Vercors, who went away seven years ago. On my word, I think you've already forgotten him.

Don't you remember that old man? He was called Anne Vercors. The master of Combernon wasn't always Jacques Hury.

JACQUES: If he comes back, he will see the farmland in good condition.

MARA: And the house too. Seven years already since he left. [*Low voice.*] I hear him coming back.

JACQUES: Not many come back from the Holy Land.

MARA: If he were alive, he would have found a way to send word to us during these seven years.

JACQUES: The Holy Land is far away. You have to cross the ocean.

MARA: There are pirates, Turks, accidents, sickness, cut-throats.

JACQUES: Right here there is plenty of evil and wickedness.

MARA: Yes, that woman, for example, who was found at the bottom of a sand pile.

JACQUES: What woman?

MARA: They say she was a leper. She might have fallen by accident. Why was she walking about? Someone might even have pushed her.

JACQUES: She was a leper?

MARA: That scares you, doesn't it? Just a bit of

[279]

leprosy is bad for the eyes. When you can't see, you shouldn't walk about. There are many who don't like to have a leper close by. Accidents have a way of happening quickly.

JACQUES: All the same, if your father does return, it isn't certain that he'll be very pleased.

MARA: He'll say right away that he always preferred Mara. And he'll be glad to know that it was she who got Jacques at the end. And that she sleeps every night beside him like a bare sword.

JACQUES: And he'll be happy, won't he, to kiss his granddaughter?

MARA: "What a beautiful child!" he'll say. "What pretty blue eyes! They remind me of something."

JACQUES [*as if he were the father*]: "And where is the mother?"

MARA [*curtsy*]: "Not here at the moment, my Lord! When people go off to Jerusalem, they shouldn't expect to find everything the same. Seven years is a long time. Now it's Mara who occupies her place at the corner of the fire."

JACQUES [*as above*]: "Good morning, Mara!"

MARA: "Good morning, father!"

> [*Anne Vercors has come in at the side of the stage and is behind them. He*

> carries in his arms the body of Vio-
> laine.]

ANNE: Good morning, Jacques!

SCENE II

[*Anne Vercors moves around the table and stands behind it at the place of the head chair. He looks at them.*] Good morning, Mara! [*She does not answer.*]

JACQUES: Father, what are you carrying under your cloak? What is that body in your arms?

ANNE: Help me to place it full length on this table. Gently, my boy, gently! [*They place the body on the table and Anne Vercors covers it with his cloak.*] This is the table where I broke bread with you on the day I left. Jacques! Mara! You are here in my place and my kingdom continues in you. It is the earth from one end to the other over which my shadow extends, like a great poplar tree at times longer and shorter at other times. I have heard what you said about my wife, and I know that she is waiting for me in that place which I shall not be long in reaching.

JACQUES: Father, I ask you what you have

[281]

brought us in your arms, and what is that dead body stretched out on the table.

ANNE: Not dead, Jacques. Not quite dead yet. Can't you see that she is breathing?

JACQUES: Who is it, father?

ANNE: Someone I found yesterday on my way. She was under a great sand pile. I heard her voice calling feebly.

JACQUES: She is a leper, isn't she?

ANNE: Yes, a leper. Who told you? You knew it already. Was it Mara who told you?

JACQUES: Could I ask you why you brought a leper into my house?

ANNE: Are you going to put the both of us out? She spoke to me and asked me to bring her here. She can still speak. But the beautiful eyes of my child Violaine have gone. She has no eyes.

JACQUES: Does she hear what we are saying?

ANNE: I don't know. She wants peace. She wants you to stop being angry with her. And Mara too, if she is angry.

[*He looks at Violaine.*]

JACQUES: I am not angry.

ANNE: She has no eyes now. But her heart still beats feebly. All night I heard the heart of

[282]

my child beat against mine. She tried to pull
me closer to her, but so feebly. Her heart
would stop from time to time and then it
would start up again its painful beat, beat, beat.

JACQUES: Did she speak to you about me?

ANNE: Yes, Jacques.

JACQUES: And about the other man too? She
was my fiancée. One morning in May he . . .

ANNE: Whom are you talking about?

JACQUES: Pierre de Craon! A leper and a thief!
He was the mason who seven years ago came to
open the flank on Monsanvierge.

[*Silence.*]

ANNE: There was no sin between Violaine and
Pierre.

JACQUES: What have you to say about the
chaste kiss she gave him on a morning in May?
[*Silence. Anne Vercors slowly shakes his head
negatively. Jacques goes to Mara and raises her
right hand.*] A morning in May. Mara swears
that on that morning, she was up early and saw
Violaine tenderly kiss Pierre de Craon on the
mouth.

[*Silence.*]

ANNE: I say no.

JACQUES: Did Mara lie, then?

[283]

ANNE: She did not lie.

JACQUES: She never allowed me to touch her, and I was her fiancée.

ANNE: I saw Pierre de Craon in Jerusalem. He was cured.

JACQUES: Cured?

ANNE: Yes. That is why he had gone there, to fulfill a vow.

JACQUES: He is cured and I am cursed!

ANNE: It is to cure you, Jacques, that I have brought you this living relic.

JACQUES: Father, I had a child who almost died. Her name is Aubaine. And she was cured.

ANNE: Thanks be to God!

JACQUES: Thanks be to God! But you had given me your daughter. She belonged to me and her mouth too and the breath of life between her lips.

ANNE: A woman's mouth is God's before it belongs to a man. On the day of baptism God puts salt in it and it is only to God that she says: Let Him kiss me with a kiss of His mouth!

JACQUES: She belonged to me. I had given her my ring.

ANNE: It's on her finger.

JACQUES [*stupefied*]: She is still wearing it?

[284]

ANNE: In Jerusalem Pierre de Craon gave it to me and I put it back on the finger of the donor.

JACQUES: And you are thinking that my ring makes a pair with Mara's.

ANNE: Show it all the more respect.

JACQUES: It was a morning in May, father. Everything around her was joyous. She loved me and I loved her. I had given her everything.

ANNE: Can't you understand, Jacques, it was too perfect. It was not acceptable.

JACQUES: What do you mean?

ANNE: The daughter was listening to the same call which the father had heard.

JACQUES: What call?

ANNE [*as if reciting*]: The Angel of God announced to Mary and she conceived by the Holy Spirit.

JACQUES: What did she conceive?

ANNE: All the suffering of the world around her, and the Church divided in two, and she saw France for whom Jeanne was burned alive! And that is why she kissed that leper, on his mouth, knowing what she did.

JACQUES: Did she decide all that in a second?

ANNE: Behold the handmaid of the Lord!

JACQUES: She saved the world and my soul is lost.

[285]

ANNE: No, Jacques is not lost, and Mara is not lost, even if she wanted to be, and Aubaine is alive. Nothing is lost. France is not lost. Between heaven and earth there is an irresistible giving out of hope and blessing. The Pope is in Rome and the King is on his throne. I was shocked because the face of the Church was darkened and because it seemed about to crumble when everyone deserted her. I wanted to press against the empty tomb, and put my hand in the hole made by the cross, as the apostle put his in the hole of the hands and the feet and the heart. Violaine was wiser. The purpose of life is not to live. The feet of the children of God are not bound to this wretched earth. It is not a question of living, but of dying. Not a question of building the cross, but hanging from it and giving what we have joyfully. That is what is meant by joy and freedom, by grace and eternal youth. The blood of an old man on the sacrificial cloth next to that of the young man makes as red a spot and as fresh as that of the first year lamb. O Violaine, child of grace, flesh of my flesh! As far as the smoking fire of the farm is from the morning star, when you rest your haloed head on the bosom of the sun, may your father in eternity see you in that place reserved for you! God grant that where the child passes, the father will too! What worth is the world by comparison with life? And what worth does life have except to be used and given? Why be tormented when it is so simple to obey and the order is clear? That is how Violaine immediately follows the hand which takes hers.

JACQUES: Cruel Violaine, whom my soul desired, you betrayed me. Hateful garden! useless scorned love, garden planted at the wrong time. Sweet perfidious Violaine! Silence and understanding of woman! Can you say nothing to me? Can you give me no answer? Will you continue to be silent? She deceived me with lying words. She deceived me with her bitter charming smile and she goes off there where I can't follow her. I have to live and go on living with this poisoned arrow in my side.

[*Noises of the farm stirring.*]

ANNE: The day is breaking. I hear the farm waking up and the cavalry of my land in its heavy harness four by four, the heavy quadriga the Bible speaks of which prepare for the gospel of the ploughshare and the sheaf.

[*He opens the large double door. Daylight enters.*]

[287]

JACQUES: Look, father! Look at the land which is yours and which was waiting for you with a smile on its lips! It is your domain. An ocean of furrows to the end of France. In my charge it has not lost its merit. At least the land did not deceive me, and I did not deceive the faithful, the powerful land. A man still runs Combernon. I have respected my marriage and my pledge with it.

ANNE: It is not the season of harvest but of sowing. The land has nourished us for long enough, and now it is time for me to nourish it [*turning toward Violaine*] with this precious seed.

JACQUES: Violaine! Can you hear me?

MARA [*violently*]: She can't hear. Your voice doesn't reach her. But she'll hear me. [*Low and threatening.*] Violaine! It is your sister. Can you hear me?

JACQUES: I saw her hand move.

MARA: You see! She does hear. She heard the voice of her sister which one Christmas day forced its way deep within her.

JACQUES: Father, she is mad! Do you hear what she is saying? That miracle of the child! I'm losing my mind.

[288]

ACT IV

ANNE: She is speaking the truth. I know the whole story.

MARA: No, I'm not mad. Look! She is hearing us. She understands. What did our father say just now? What does the first bell of the angelus say?

ANNE: "The Angel of God announced to Mary and she conceived by the Holy Spirit."

MARA: And what does the second bell say?

ANNE: "Behold the handmaid of the Lord. So be it according to Your will."

MARA: And the third bell?

ANNE: "And the Word was made flesh and dwelt among us."

MARA: And the Word was made flesh and dwelt among us. Mara's cry, her call, her scream also became flesh in the breast of this horror, in the breast of her enemy, in the breast of this ruined woman, in the breast of this abominable leper. From the depth of my being I cried so loud that finally I snatched away from her that child she had taken from me. I snatched away from this living tomb the child that was mine and she gave birth to it.

JACQUES: She did that?

MARA: Yes, you know the story. On Christmas eve I told you that Aubaine was sick. Well, she

[289]

was dead at that time. Her body was cold. But you say she did that. It was God who did it. I was stronger than she was. I did it!

> [*Jacques utters a cry and pushing Mara aside, falls at the feet of Violaine.*]

MARA: He falls on his knees before Violaine who betrayed him for a leper. She was too good for this earth which is good enough for the rest of us! She had given her word, and with her lips she put that word between the lips of a leper . . .

JACQUES: Stop talking!

MARA: Violaine is the only one he loves. She is the only one they all love. Her father left her and her mother too who used to advise her, and her fiancé who once believed in her. That was the extent of their love. Mine is different.

JACQUES: You are right. I know now it was you who led Violaine to the sand pile. One hand led her and the other pushed her.

MARA: So, nothing escapes you.

JACQUES: Am I right or wrong?

MARA: Is it right that the man who belongs to me be cut in two, one half here and the other in the forest of Chevoche? Is it right that the child who belongs to me be cut in two and have two mothers, one for her body and the other for her soul? Yes, I did it!

ANNE: No, Mara, it wasn't you. It was the demon who possessed you. You are suffering. I want to help you. I've come back now and I'll be your father now forever, the same father you used to love. You and Violaine are my two little girls, my two children I hold in my arms. I loved both of you. Your two hearts beat with mine when I hold you.

MARA [*with a cry*]: Father, my child was dead and she brought her back to life!

CHILD'S VOICE [*outside*]:

> Marguerite of Paris
> Lend me your gray slippers
> To go to Paradise!
> How beautiful the world!
> How warm it is!
> I hear the bird
> Go pip! pip! pip!

[*In the middle of the song Violaine raises her arm and lets it fall beside Jacques.*]

VIOLAINE: It's a pretty song, father. I recognize it. We used to sing it when we went to get blackberries in the hedge, Mara and I.

[291]

ANNE: Jacques is here, close to you.

VIOLAINE: Is he still angry?

ANNE: He's over being angry.

VIOLAINE [*putting her hand on his head*]: Good morning, Jacques!

JACQUES [*thickly*]: Greetings to my fiancée through the flowering branches!

VIOLAINE: Father, tell him I love him.

ANNE: He has never stopped loving you.

VIOLAINE: Father, tell him I love him.

ANNE: Listen to him. He says nothing.

VIOLAINE: Pierre de Craon . . .

ANNE: What about him?

VIOLAINE: Tell Pierre de Craon that I love him. With that kiss I gave him he must make a church.

ANNE: It's already begun.

VIOLAINE: And Mara loves me. She's the only one who believed in me.

ANNE: Listen to her now, Jacques.

VIOLAINE: The child she gave me, the child that was born in my arms. Oh Mara! she was so good and obedient. Everything she did was just right. What a wonderful thing, father, what a terrible thing it is to give birth to another soul in the world!

[292]

ANNE: Do you mean this world or another world?

VIOLAINE: There are two, but I say there is only one and that is enough, and the mercy of God is boundless.

JACQUES: Happiness is something real for me.

VIOLAINE: What difference does it make? Happiness was never promised you. Work. That is what is asked of you. If you question this old land, it will answer you with bread and wine. I have finished with it and am going on. What is one day when we are not together? Soon it will be passed. And then your turn will come and you will see the big door open. I will be on the other side, close by.

JACQUES: Greetings to my fiancée through the flowering branches!

VIOLAINE: You remember that, Jacques? Now you must carry me away from here.

JACQUES: Carry you away?

VIOLAINE: This isn't the place for a leper to die. Carry me to that shelter my father had built for the poor at the gate of Monsanvierge. [*Jacques prepares to lift her.*] No, not you, Jacques.

JACQUES: Not even this last duty?

VIOLAINE: I want my father. I put my spirit back into the arms of my father. [*Silence. Anne Vercors takes the wrist of Violaine and slowly counts with the left hand, his eyes lowered.*] Are you still here, Jacques?

JACQUES: I am here.

VIOLAINE: Has it been a good year? Does the wheat look beautiful?

JACQUES: There is so much, we don't know where to put it.

VIOLAINE: There is nothing more beautiful than a great harvest. Yes, even now I can remember how it looks.

JACQUES: Yes, Violaine.

VIOLAINE: How wonderful it is to be alive! How boundless the glory of God!

JACQUES: You must live and stay with us.

VIOLAINE [*falls back*]: But it is also good to die when everything is over, when the darkness slowly spreads over us like a very dark shadow. [*Silence.*]

ANNE: She won't say anything more.

JACQUES: Take her. She is yours. Take her to where she said. She doesn't want me to touch her. Gently! Very gently!

[*Anne Vercors leaves with the body.*

[294]

Jacques Hury follows him with his eyes.]

THE ANGELUS [*voice*]: Pax pax pax.

VOICES: Gloria in excelsis Deo et in terra pax
hominibus bonae voluntatis Laetare

Laetare

Laetare

[*During this, while Jacques watches
Anne Vercors who goes off with the
body of Violaine, Mara comes forward
with her child. Jacques slowly turns
back to her. Mara raises her child and
with her makes the sign of the cross.
Jacques turns his head a moment to the
road where Anne has disappeared. Then
to Mara. They look at one another during the final notes of the angelus . . .*

[*Silence.*]

Since 1939 all the important dramas of Paul Claudel have been produced and played by the greatest names of the French theater. Parisian audiences have gathered in their theaters for the celebrated ritual of judgment and have discovered and declared—not, of course, without the usual Gallic controversy—that here indeed was great drama. In England, T. S. Eliot announced himself in similar fashion by hailing Claudel as the greatest poetic dramatist of our century. This book offers the English-reading public two of Claudel's most significant works: *Break of Noon* in its first English translation; *The Tidings Brought to Mary* in its first new translation in more than thirty years.

BREAK OF NOON

A drama in three acts. It is perhaps the most awesome of all Claudel's dramas and the closest to pure tragedy. There are four characters—three men and a woman —a few voices producing a great variety of moods and tempi. The principal theme is adultery and the secondary theme is the struggle in a man between a religious vocation and sexual love. The woman, Ysé, seeks from the three men—her husband and two lovers—a stability that no one can give her and that she will find only in death. She speaks and loves within her